MW01415199

plugin**turn**on

plugin**turn**on
a guide to internet filmmaking

Ana **Kronschnabl**
& Tomas **Rawlings**

First published in Great Britain and in the USA in 2004 by
MARION BOYARS PUBLISHERS LTD
24 Lacy Road, London SW15 1NL

www.marionboyars.co.uk

Distributed in Australia and New Zealand by Peribo Pty Ltd
58 Beaumont Road, Kuring-gai, NSW 2080

Printed in 2004
10 9 8 7 6 5 4 3 2 1

A CIP catalogue record for this book is available from the British Library.
A CIP catalog record for this book is available from the Library of Congress.

ISBN 0-7145-3102-2

Set in Elegant Garamond 11.5/14pt
Printed in Great Britain by Biddles, King's Lynn.

ACKNOWLEDGMENTS

Thanks to: Chaz Bocock, Daniel Keeble, Hugh Hancock, John Honniball, Lev Manovich, Stephen Marshall, Robert Newman, Nicola, Pomegranate (of Infoshop Helpers), Shaun Saville, Richard Stallman, Michael Stutz, Stu Collier, Stu Griffin, Mike White and all the crew at Marion Boyars Publishers.

With special thanks to Armin Elsaesser for all his help and support.

This book is dedicated to George, filmmaking inspiration for over twenty years, to all the people who have contributed to plugincinema's success over the last five years and to the future of web filmmaking!

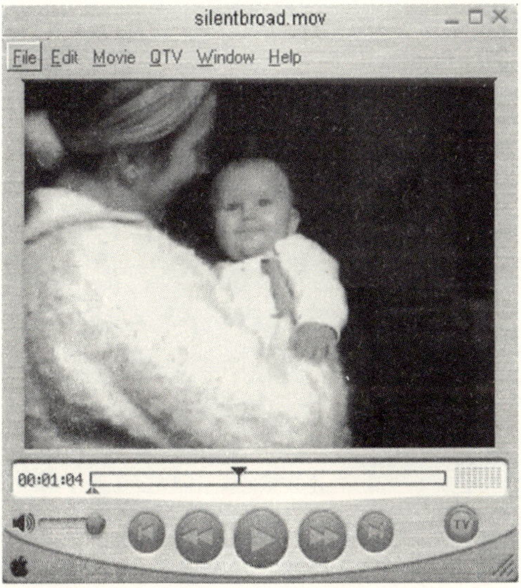

***Silent Night*, plugincinema.com, 2002 (QuickTime)**

CONTENTS

THINKING

Foreword by Lev Manovich 11
Introduction to Filmmaking for the Internet 17
Chapter 1: The Revolution Will be Digitized 25
Chapter 2: File Format Wars 37
Chapter 3: The Rights and Wrongs of Copyright 47
Chapter 4: Business at the Speed of Light 61
Chapter 5: The Pluginmanifesto 77

DOING

Foreword by Robert Newman 89
Chapter 6: From Idea to Online 91
Chapter 7: The Production Process 99
Chapter 8: Tools of the Trade 107
Chapter 9: Advice on Cameras 119
Chapter 10: Compression 125
Chapter 11: Using the Internet as a Cinema 135
Chapter 12: A Practical Manifesto 151
A Final Note by Ana Kronschnabl 163

APPENDICES

Introduction to Appendices 167
Appendix I: A Sample Script and Storyboard 169
Appendix II: Capturing Digital Footage 177
Appendix III: Basic Editing With VirtualDubMod 183
Appendix IV: Distributing Film on a File Trade Network 197
Appendix V: Encoding Using QuickTimePro 5 205
Appendix VI: Creating a Webpage for Free 213
Appendix VII: Using Paypal to Accept Money Over the Internet 231

GLOSSARY 243
INDEX 251

THINKING

Foreword to 'Thinking' by Lev Manovich

One of Marshall McLuhan's more accessible insights was the idea that, from the outset, each new medium imitates a previous one. The first book printed by Gutenberg closely imitated illustrated books created by hand at the time; similarly, during its first couple of decades, cinema closely imitated theatre. On my cynical days, I wonder if his insight should be re-written in the following way: in a global media society, each new media is extensively used to sell the already existing one. So, for instance, in the case of films on the net, so far filmmakers typically use the net simply to advertise their 'normal' films through websites and trailers – rather than creating original films specifically for the net.

But what would a truly net-specific cinema look like? This question is not an easy one to answer. This is because with a digital computer, McLuhan's insight no longer works. We expect that each new media first imitates older media and eventually develops its own unique language. But by definition, a digital computer is a simulation machine. In other words, its identity is that it does not have any identity of its own. Indeed, this is how British mathematician Alan Turing defined digital computer already in the 1930s: a computer is a new kind of virtual machine which can simulate almost any other machine. Turing was not explicitly thinking about the simulation of other media. However, when later in the 1970s Alan Kay and his colleagues at Xerox developed the modern graphical user interface along with the first software for painting, word-processing, animation and so on, the computer became the first metamedium (the term actually used by Kay), capable of simulating all existing media as well as their previously non-existent combinations.

In a certain sense, the history of digital computing runs in a direction that is exactly opposite to the normal evolution of a new media – i.e. from imitation to the development of an original language – and appears to be systematically reversing this normal direction. Recall that at first, in the 1940s and 1950s, people had to painstakingly program room-size computers in their original machine language. Later, high-level programming languages such as Fortran, Cobol, 'C' and others made programming easier by allowing the machine to pretend that it understood instructions similar to those of natural languages. A little later still, the graphical user interface made the computer even more of a media simulator: the computer was now able to pretend that it was an office desktop with folders, trashcan, etc. (using the now familiar 'desktop' metaphor).

Today the computer seems to be moving even closer towards completely 'disappearing' in favour of simulating old media. For instance, some research prototypes for a digital book imagine it as something which looks very much like a normal book or magazine, except that the content of the pages can actually change dynamically rather than being static (so a new book can be uploaded from the net at any time onto these pages). Luckily for an aspiring net filmmaker, this paradox is a false one. Think again about such an electronic book, which looks like a traditional book – except that all its pages have the functionality of a dynamic, net-connected, interactive computer screen. Despite superficial physical similarity to a paper-based book, such an electronic book is something completely different – just as any webpage on the net today is fundamentally different from an old-fashioned printed page. In short, the basic law of computer metamedium may be formulated in this way: simulation on one area goes hand in hand with revolution in another. Or, when we simulate a media in a computer, we fundamentally change it into something new.

Once we adopt this perspective, it is easy to notice it at work in other areas of digital culture. Think for instance about the elusive promise of 'interactive narrative.' Despite all the hype and experiments in this direction in the last twenty years, it seems to me that 'interactive narrative' never really happened on any significant scale. What we have instead is a very mature cultural form of the computer game phenomenon, with its various genres, conventions and cultures. There is also the much more limited and yet also very important interactivity of DVDs, where the user can go to any scene of a movie, watch the 'making of' and even sometimes select which camera view is shown. Digital Video Recorders (DVR) too, allow interactivity; enabling consumers to turn television from a linear medium into a media database that they can access when they want and in any order they want.

The emergence of DVRs may sound like a trivial event, but historically it is a very important development. In the 1990s all the discussions around 'interactive narrative' were fundamentally elitist, but today millions of people use DVDs and DVRs. Logically these technologies make perfect sense. They represent a particular stage in the computerization of culture, where the already established economic/cultural forms such as linear feature films and linear television programming are slowly being broken apart into their constitutive elements. In short, while they may appear to be simply new distribution technologies, DVD and DVR are in fact quite revolutionary in their effects on the content they distribute; systematically taking it apart into its elements. This to me seems to be a necessary and healthy development: a required stage before we get to some completely new forms such as 'interactive narrative.' (Note that a similar 'legolization' – the term I made up from Lego – is happening in the music industry. If previously a record or a CD was the industry unit, today under the influence of online music stores such as the iTunes store, the new unit is a single track or song.)

So far we have been talking about what happens inside a screen, so to speak, and yet slowly the very concept of screen, which forms the foundation of modern cinema, is also changing into something quite different. Once again, these changes are slow, combining simulation of what already exists with revolutionary developments. What I am talking about is the new stage in the history of computing, which can be described using already established terms such as 'ubiquitous computing' and 'ambient intelligence', or maybe new terms will become necessary. The bottom line is that computation, telecommunication and interface are slowly being incorporated into a variety of objects and spaces, rather than being confined to particular types of objects such as desktop computers or a telephone. So I think that slowly our concept of an object as something 'dead' and 'passive' will change, as more and more objects will become 'smart' and 'net-aware.' So one day, traditional 'dump' objects may become an exception rather than the norm. In the same manner, if today dynamic screens constitute a small percentage of any surfaces in any space, one day every surface may potentially function as a screen connected to networks.

This future is closer than you may think. Nissan design studio located in San Diego where I teach has already developed a prototype car shown in the 2004 Detroit Car Show in which the whole ceiling of the car interior functioned as a screen, programmable by the driver.

We live in an interesting period in which science fiction has seemingly caught up with the present. We no longer have to travel to distant planets in search of new alien civilizations, because our own planet is rapidly turning into one. This gives the net filmmaker both unprecedented creative possibilities as well as a very serious responsibility – helping us navigate this new alien universe.

Lev Manovich is Associate Professor at the Visual Arts Department, University of California, San Diego and is author of *The Language of New Media* (M.I.T. Press, 2001).

An Introduction to Filmmaking for the Internet

A History of the Future

This book is about web filmmaking: the brash offspring of networked technology and digital media. Although immature, web filmmaking's growth has been rapid, with hints of a nascent potential. Whilst most films have until recently been widely available for consumption only, web films are also accessible in terms of production and distribution – and herein lies the unique promise that web filmmaking offers its enthusiasts. In order to map out this trajectory, we would like to look back over this brief history and pull out some of the salient moments.

The year is 1995: Barings Bank collapses losing over £600 million (brought down by rogue futures trader Nick Leeson), amidst much fanfare Microsoft is on the march with the Windows 95 operating system and Sony is busy unveiling their entry into the world of computer games – The Playstation. Amidst all this excitement, most people have failed to notice a piece of software called StreamWorks developed by a small company called Xing Technology Corporation. This technology is considered by many to be the original live and on-demand audio/video delivery system for the internet.[1] It was the first mass-market streaming media software; history was being made.

The year is 1998: people across the world are watching the machinations of the Bill Clinton/Monica Lewinsky sex scandal unfold, Microsoft is launching its updated operating system, Windows 98, and an artificially intelligent cuddly toy known as 'Furby' is high on the shopping list of the western world. *Shift* magazine rated this year as ninth in its list of the ten most defining moments in digital culture. They stated that, 'The internet, though very much in its infancy compared to other mass mediums, has still managed to have many of its own seminal moments.'[2] This ninth moment heralded the debut of a short film called *Troops*. If you have not seen the film, it is an accomplished and witty parody that mixes the format of the US TV show *Cops*, with the characters and setting of *Star Wars*. Director Kevin Rubio and his friends had produced a landmark of digital culture: 'Shot for a measly $1,200 (US), the short – *Troops* – had eye-popping special effects generated on Rubio's home computers. He posted it online, and just like that, gazillions of *Star Wars* nuts stampeded over to download it. Rubio found he'd created a new meme overnight...'[3] Many hailed *Troops* and the movement of which it was a part, as proof of the democratization of film.[4]

It was the year after this that plugincinema itself was launched – at the 1999 Brief Encounters short film festival in Bristol, England. For the last five years, plugincinema has existed to show, discuss, debate and enable the creation of online films. As the seed of the venture is a PhD research project, plugincinema was always driven by an enquiring mindset and remained firmly focused on onlinefilms. This book is the result of five years of such thinking and practice.

Today, audio and video content are now a ubiquitous part of the internet. A 2003 study by Arbitron Inc., the international media and marketing research firm, showed that a significant number of Americans (around 20%) have used the internet to consume media in the last month.[5] Xing Technology Corporation is now a small part of the media conglomerate RealNetworks.[6] There are now so many *Star Wars* fan films made that they have their own awards ceremony.[7] Media content on the internet seems to have come of age. However, this growth has invited a number of questions. On the plugincinema website, for example, the question was raised whether it was adequate that this blossoming new medium should become merely a low-quality (in all senses of the word) version of TV or film in its current format.

Upgrading the Media

To understand this new medium better we have broken it down into smaller bite-sized (or byte-sized!) chunks. Firstly, we would suggest that there are broadly three forms of films that can be encountered on the internet:

- Films made for traditional promotional purposes.
- Films not made for, but distributed via the internet.
- Web films.

Examining the characteristics of these broad forms enables us to consider the larger questions around internet based media technology.

Form:	**Description:**	**Defining Features:**	**Example:**
Films made for traditional promotional purposes.	A digitized version of films shot with the same production methods and technology used for TV/Cinema.	Often 35mm (the standard size for celluloid film) or high quality digital footage.[8] (Usually highly compressed.)	Cinema trailers online, for example the trailer for *Lord of the Rings*.[9]
Films not made for, but distributed via the internet.	A film taking advantage of the internet for distribution.	Often large files and/or designed to be downloaded not streamed. Highly compressed versions of pirated films.	The short film *405 The Movie* (the story of a jet liner landing on a freeway).[10]
Web films.	Films made with the medium of the internet and its constraints in mind.	Made in harmony with internet and computer technologies such as streaming or Flash or After Effects.[11]	The short film *Distance Over Time* (an experiment in filmmaking using lo-fi technology to make a visual and audio collage).[12]

This book focuses primarily on the third form, web films, because we consider web films to be, potentially, a unique new form of media. Although it has things in common with both the cinema and TV, web filmmaking differs, since the environment for both the creation and distribution of web films is entirely new.

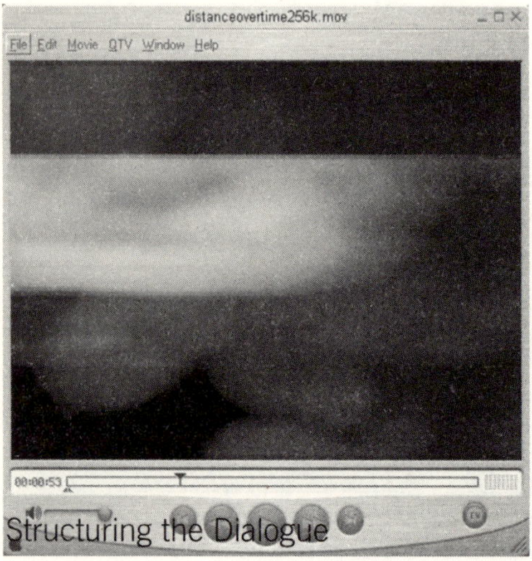

***Distance Over Time*, Dir. Ana Kronschnabl, 2003 (QuickTime)**

The chapters in this book fall into two sections – 'Thinking' and 'Doing' – and each section includes an extensive list of references to the source material, as well as a list of web links that can be used to explore each subject area in greater detail.

This book can be used in two ways: as a complete guide, being read from beginning to end, or in a similar way to a cookbook, where each chapter is a self-contained recipe that can be dipped into as needed. It has been written and cross-referenced in such a way that the reader can access the information needed to fully understand each chapter without having to read the book in its entirety.

Knowledge is Power

'Thinking' outlines some of the issues surrounding the creation of media for the internet: it's about the ideas that are driving this emerging technology and the players that are carrying them to the surface; it's about empowering the filmmaker to understand both what is happening and why it is happening. We believe that this knowledge is vital to understanding the web filmmaking landscape, how to traverse it and how to work within it. Any filmmaker intending a foray into online culture without an understanding of the digital environment is as reckless as an explorer setting off into the tropics without a map! (Although perhaps not as vulnerable…)

Making it Happen

'Doing' aims to provide a level of technical information that will enable a filmmaker to fully engage with this new medium. Whilst no one book could fully cover the plethora of computers, cameras, internet connections, software and hardware involved in making a film, we have tried to demystify these technologies and also recommend a number of books, magazines and internet sites that can help guide a first time filmmaker in their choice of equipment, as research is needed to ensure that the everything you opt for is compatible.

Just the Beginning

Hollywood does not have to be the pinnacle of a filmmaker's career. We are not suggesting a movement in response to Hollywood but a movement separate from it: we are not reacting against Hollywood but engaging in our own creation. This is not the traditional knee-jerk response to the mainstream but a genuinely original movement with motivations and pre-occupations that are completely unique, although rooted, as is all multimedia, in the filmmaking annals. If digital technology offers us anything, it is the possibility of control over how we engage with the entire filmmaking process. We have within our grasp the opportunity to make, edit and disseminate our own work. What is even more exciting is that this is just the beginning of what digital technology has to offer us...

Links for Further Thinking

Note: This book will provide a number of links to the internet. There are two points to remember about these links if you are typing them in. Firstly, these website links do not have spaces in them, where there is a gap between words or characters it will have an underscore symbol there (_) so 'www.sample.com/web' address will actually be typed in as 'www.sample.com/web_address'. Also, some websites do not need the 'www' bit (just type 'http://') and the address) and some will add 'http://' automatically (just type 'www').

'Films Note on the Internet: An Introduction'
http://www.plugincinema.com/plugin/film_school/onlinefilm.htm

Distance Over Time on plugincinema.com
http://www.plugincinema.com/plugin/plugin_cinema/index.htm#f28

plugincinema discussion of the web filmmaking aesthetic
http://www.plugincinema.com/plugin/plugin_aesthetic

405 The Movie
http://www.405themovie.com

Cinema Trailers Online
http://www.apple.com/trailers

Star Wars Fan Film *Troops*
http://www.theforce.net/theater/shortfilms/troops

Xing Technology Corporation
http://www.real.com/accessories/?prod=xingmp3encoder

References and Notes

1 '...streaming media entered the internet in 1995 with its first delivery system by Xing Technology.' **http://web.ptc.org/library/proceedings/ptc2000/sessions/monday/m35/m352**

2 **http://www.shift.com/content/10.3/398/1.html**

3 **http://www.shift.com/content/10.3/398/2.html**

4 So says Henry Jenkins, Director of the Comparative Media Studies Program, Massachusetts Institute of Technology. **http://web.mit.edu/21fms/www/faculty/henry3/starwars.html**

5 Source is a study entitled 'Internet and Multimedia 11: New Media Enters the Mainstream.' **http://www.webcasters.org/news/20030924.htm**

6 RealNetworks acquired Xing Technology in 1999. **http://www.wired.com/wired/archive/7.08/dl_timeline.html**

7 Called 'The Star Wars Fan Film Awards.' **http://atomfilms.shockwave.com/af/spotlight/collections/starwars/**

8 If you are interested in shooting High Definition footage, see the GR-HD1 from JVC, the world's first high-definition camcorder for consumers. **http://www.gizmodo.com/archives/006542.php**

9 *The Lord of the Rings* trailers can be found at **http://www.lordoftherings.net**

10 *405 The Movie* can be found at **http://www.405themovie.com**

11 Flash is a web-specific interactivity and animation creation tool. For more information on Flash, see Chapter 8. After Effects is compositing, animation and effects software produced by Adobe, more information can be found at **http://www.adobe.com/products/aftereffects/main.html**

12 The film *Distance Over Time* can be found on plugincinema.com **http://www.plugincinema.com/plugin/plugin_cinema/index.htm#f28**

Chapter 1: The Revolution Will be Digitized

Ownership and Distribution in the Internet Age

Technologically rooted language is commonplace. Whilst we might not all understand the exact process that a word or phrase represents, the terms we use for the most practical applications are quickly assimilated into everyday language use. One such word is MP3. To many people MP3 has become a byword for music stored in a digital format, though it is only one method of storing digital music, and others include .wav, .aif etc. However, MP3 is a particularly efficient form of music compression (see Chapter 10) that enables the user to take a music track (taking around 35 megabytes to store) and reduce it by about a tenth (to around 3.5 megabytes). This compressed form of music is called MP3 (or to be more exact 'Mpeg-1 Audio Layer-3').[1] This technology has transformed the way people exchange music, since even a standard 56K modem connection can transfer an MP3 music track from the internet onto a person's hard-drive in less than 20 minutes.[2] (The most common method of connecting a computer to the internet today is via a modem that uses a normal phone line to dial out. The names of these modems are synonymous with the speed at which they can transmit information to and from the internet, a 56K version being the ceiling limit of this technology. Its full title is a 56,000 bps modem, bps being 'bits per second'.) When you combine this technology with the now ubiquitous CD burner, the home-user can download music, burn it to CD and then play it on most home music systems within the space of a few minutes – depending on the file size of course.

Although the technology has now raced ahead, when it first emerged in Germany back in 1987 web-users who wanted to take full advantage of this new distribution method needed sources of MP3s.[3] Music files were soon being posted on the internet, with fans trading new singles and album tracks from a whole variety of artists. However, although many were of non-copyrighted material, most were the copyrighted property of record companies and they were not happy. Websites carrying these tracks soon found themselves on the receiving end of a legal ultimatum – remove any copyrighted material or be sued. It was becoming apparent that the legal definitions of ownership had not kept up with the consumers' use of technology.

Then in 1995 an Australian teenager, Adam Hinkley, created an application called 'Hotline', which allowed people to trade files without needing websites.[4] Hotline was a powerful application that was immediately successful amongst the technologically literate, especially hackers and digital pirates, yet it would take another four years before the rest of the world would wake up to the technological revolution that this programme had unleashed.

The Napster Challenge

In June 1999 Shawn Fanning launched the now infamous application we know as 'Napster,' and like most great ideas, its power was in its simplicity. The Napster Network acted as a go-between, enabling users to view each other's music. It did not store the music files, it was the facilitator, simply hooking users up to each other. Here is how a basic exchange worked:

1. User A logs on to the network and searches for 'Nirvana'.
2. Napster knows from its cataloguing activity of all of its users that User B has a large collection and is currently online. (*Note*: User B would have previously told the Napster software which directory on their computer it is OK to share files from, as

opposed to those which are private.)

3. Napster gives User A the list of files from User B's personal computer.
4. User A then copies the desired music files from computer to computer.

Simple, especially when you multiply this by the millions of users on the network and the billions of music files they have to share, which greatly improves a person's chances of finding the music they are seeking. Napster was also a very powerful idea with far reaching implications. The perfect application for the internet age, it was a distribution system of incredible efficiency and diversity; a music library composed of millions of music lover's individual collections…and the more people who joined, the more music there was available…

The impact was of course sensational. Almost overnight the service threatened traditional music distribution. Through word-of-mouth millions signed up and began exchanging music and copyrighted material flooded the system with music from every genre – from mainstream releases to obscure studio outtakes. If we take the example of alternative rock band Radiohead, a quick search on a file-trade network not only reveals the albums they have released but also provides a live recording of the band performing a cover of U2's 'Sunday Bloody Sunday'. I also had the lead singer Thom Yorke performing alongside other musicians on a radio show. Ironically, the person who digitized this track has even included a portion of the show's outro where the host remarks, '…one day don't be surprised if...you find, like, a bootleg of that…' The balance of power had altered dramatically, giving the consumer unparalleled access to the kind of exchanges they had only hitherto dreamed about. Unsurprisingly, it was not long before the music industry became aware of the Napster phenomenon and its system, by now known as 'peer-to-peer'. (Unlike previous websites that physically stored the copyrighted materials, Napster was only the agent mediating the exchange; it never held or stored the potentially illegal files.) Initiated through the Recording Industry Association of America (RIAA), a monstrous legal and PR battle was waged that involved a huge range of people including web-users, students, colleges, the metal band Metallica, politicians, cyber-rights activists and the German media giant Bertelsmann.

The End of Copyright?

In July 2002, as the fight intensified, a group of musicians also joined the fray. They pleaded on their website: 'If a Song Means a Lot to You, Imagine What it Means to Us.'[5] This statement came from the 'Coalition for the Future of Music', a campaign to stop digital copying which was reminiscent of the 'Home Taping is Killing Music' campaign that started in the 70s.

On the other side of the debate, Napster's supporters were equally strident. Richard Stallman, founder of the Free Software Foundation (FSF), summed up his position as follows: '...people have the fundamental right to do non-commercial verbatim no-fee copying and redistribution, and stopping them, whether by law or by technical measures, is immoral. Laws prohibiting people from sharing are just as illegitimate as the apartheid laws and breaking them is not wrong.'[6]

As peer-to-peer technology began to give record company executives sleepless nights, it also posed an integral and extremely interesting question – could copyright become unenforceable and therefore irrelevant? With millions of people across the globe now exchanging tunes via the internet attempts to regulate the existing laws of copyright may prove to be virtually impossible. As a result, record companies may no longer be able to rely on simply selling music as their main source of revenue, and may need to look for other ways to provide a profit for their shareholders. This could even mean that the music business as we know it may cease to exist. Chuck D, frontman of rap group Public Enemy and now spokesman for the MP3 site RapStation, believes the future holds, '.a million artists with a million labels.'[7] Unfortunately, these sentiments did not save Napster, which was brought to its knees by protracted litigation in 2002[8] and was eventually sold off at a very modest price to the CD burning software firm Roxio.[9] Unsurprisingly, Roxio purchased all the Napster assets without the liabilities and MTV are now rumoured to be making a documentary about the meteoric rise and fall of Shawn Fanning and his Napster rebellion.

However, rather than putting paid to this activity of individuals sharing music via the net, the killing of Napster, the RIAA's 'Public Enemy Number 1', may well have had the opposite effect to that which was intended. Although Napster was not physically hosting the music, since it was the central point through which illegal music was being traded, following a protracted legal battle (lasting three years) it was judged by various courts to be culpable. This was Napster's 'Achilles heel' and though it may not have survived the battle that was raging furiously around it, the technological revolution it helped to unleash evolved to steer a different course – a course that would take note of its predecessor's mistakes. Before long, the Open Source community took the idea and ran with it. 'Open Source' defines an ideology that has no faith in the idea of copyright, its supporters make all the programming code that they produce available for all to use and modify, providing the same ideals are then adhered to by any new users. What this community produced were peer-to-peer networks with a fragmented administrative infrastructure; every user, in addition to being the storage point for the MP3 files, also became a link in the administrative web. This meant that there was no Napster-like head for the RIAA to target and therefore no technology licenses that could be owned. As one user on the technology news website slashdot.org remarked at the time: 'With these releases, it looks like the future is once again rosy in the MP3-world.'

Sales Curves

As a result of these developments, the music industry is still waging its ongoing battle against peer-to-peer networks. However, rather than focus on the theoretical issue of whether 'Napster-style' distribution of music is inherently wrong or not, some commentators are more concerned with the more practical question – does this technology actually affect DVD and CD sales? Some argue that services like Napster act as nothing more than a giant promotional tool, allowing fans to sample all kinds of music for free, but if this is true then why is the music industry not embracing the technology? In the early days of pop, in order to protect music industry revenue from record sales the playing of singles on the radio was banned. As music writer David Sinclair noted recently, '...it was also widely believed that playing records on the radio too often would actually discourage people from buying those records. After all, went the argument, if you can hear them on the radio for free, why bother to go out and buy them?'[10] The fact that music sales do seem to be dropping may appear to support these concerns, however, apportioning the blame is extremely difficult. The RIAA believes it is because of MP3 piracy but some have suggested that the industry is not producing music that consumers care enough about to buy. Others point to the increased competition for the consumer purse, speculating that factors outside the control of the industry, such as spending on mobile phones, computer games and such like, are eating into the spending power of consumers. Jupiter Research concluded that the very pirates the industry had targeted – on college campuses and through individual lawsuits – were more likely to increase their music purchases.[11] As one critic noted on MP3 usage: '...it puts another chink in the industry's already hopelessly self-serving argument that people shouldn't be able to freely exchange music now in the same way they exchanged tapes and records in the pre-digital era. If there's no profit involved, of course sharing is appropriate. The industry, not the public, should be forced to adjust.'[12] After all, home taping did not kill music.

Enter Film

The next logical step for peer-to-peer networks was to trade other forms of data, not just music, thus opening the new networks up to exchanges of written text, pictures, games and films. Until very recently the world of film had been immune to the problems that have beset the music industry. Film, comprising both sound and image, makes very large files when digitized onto a computer. The cost and time involved in storing and transmitting these files has meant that trading films over the internet has been beyond the resources of all but the most determined web-user. But in the same way that the technological advances of MP3 compression shrunk music files, so similar advances offered the possibility of doing the same with film. This factor, coupled with the spread of high-speed web connections like ADSL and Broadband, soon opened film up to the same distribution and piracy issues as the music industry. Technology, it seems, has caught up with Hollywood and unsurprisingly not everyone is happy about this. Many leading industry figures in Hollywood, for example, are concerned that a Napster-like system for films might ultimately lead to consumers ceasing to buy cinema tickets, videos or DVDs. Vince Van Petten, Executive Director of the Producers' Guild of America, remarked, 'You have a serious, serious problem when it becomes easy to download movies. That's why we are relying so heavily on digital rights management and security.'[13] The film industry has the benefit of the music industry's experience. They can, and in some cases do, see the technology advancing upon them. At present the signals are mixed: DVD sales are up ($12.1 billion in the US alone for 2002[14]) even though popular films such as *Harry Potter* and *Lord of the Rings* have been available to download from the web even before their cinema releases.

DivX: The MP3 of Film

So what types of technology are giving Hollywood such a headache? One of the front-runners is DivX. It was originally based on the Windows Media Codec, which is a bit of software that compresses and decompresses movie files. The author of the DivX codec, Jerome Rota, claims that Microsoft made him do it; a new version of Windows Media Player failed to play some footage he had compressed using an earlier piece of Microsoft software and whilst solving his compatibility problem DivX was born. In an interview with the online magazine Salon.com he stated, 'I set the information free... It only took about a week.'[15] It seems incredible that one person, in just one week, could create such a potential threat to the film industry. As Salon remarked, 'One week, one program and a potential revolution in digital video. DivX shrinks video to about a fifth of its original size, making it possible to download a full-length movie from the net to your hard drive in less than an hour.' [16]

However, unlike the emergent Napster, the people behind DivX have decided to take a different route. As the technology develops, those behind DivX are helping the film industry to explore legal forms of distribution. Users may have a different story to tell, the download rate of the new legal version of DivX has been far less than that of the unregulated version.[14]

What does this type of technology mean to filmmakers? For independent filmmakers, access to Napster-style networks could both provide distribution channels as well as an income. Maybe the future for many creative art forms, film included, lies in distribution models that are at odds with the way Hollywood or the music industry wants to do business? To some, this new model of distribution has revolutionary overtones. John Perry Barlow, co-founder of the Electronic Frontier Foundation, wrote in *Wired* magazine October 2000: 'What's happening with global, peer-to-peer networking is not altogether different from what happened when the American colonists realized they were poorly served by the British Crown. The colonists were obliged to cast off that power and develop an economy better suited to their new environment.'[17]

Links for Further Thinking

Coalition for the Future of Music
http://www.futureofmusic.com

Electronic Frontier Foundation
http://www.eff.org

Free Software Foundation
http://www.fsf.org

DivX Networks
http://www.divxnetworks.com

MP3 Pages on Wired.com
http://www.wired.com/news/mp3

RapStation
http://www.rapstation.com

References and Notes

1 See Chapter 10.

2 For more on 56K modems see the plugincinema article 'Connecting to the Internet 101'. http://www.plugincinema.com/plugin/film_school/guide_to_internet.htm

3 See http://www.zdnetindia.com/help/stories/16218.html

4 Documented in Shift.com's article 'The Defining Moments in Digital Culture.' http://www.shift.com/content/10.3/398/1.html

5 http://www.wired.com/news/politics/0,1283,37516,00.html

6 From an interview for this book dated 2003. For more information see the Free Software Foundation website http://www.fsf.org

7 http://sheila.inessential.com/2000/06/15

8 See http://www.wired.com/news/business/0,1367,5232,00.html

9 See http://www.wired.com/news/digiwood/o,01412,58895,00.html

10 Re-quoted from an earlier plugincinema article 'The Revolution Will Be Digitized: MP3, Napster & Hollywood'. http://www.plugincinema.com/plugin/articles/mp3_1.htm

11 See CNet article http://news.com.com/2100-1023-243463.html?legacy=cnet

12 See USA Today editorial/opinion piece from 5th June 2002. http://www.usatoday.com/news/opinion/2002/05/07/edtwof.htm

13 Quoted in a *Wired* article. http://www.wired.com/news/business/0,1367,41385,00.html

14 Figures from DVD Entertainment Group, quoted by Rediff.com. http://www.rediff.com/entertai/2003/jan/10dvd.htm

15 http://www.salon.com/tech/feature/2001/03/15/divx_part1/index.html

16 'Only 500,000 people have downloaded the new version of DivX, DivX ;-) Deux, and most of the movies available online _

including *Snatch* and others that have been released since the appearance of the upgraded DivX software – still flow only through the original DivX.'
http://dir.salon.com/tech/feature/2001/03/19/divx_part2/index.html

17 http://www.wardrum.org/awareness/truth/10_02_4.html

Chapter 2: File Format Wars

The Hidden War

Unbeknownst to most people, the software they use to access the internet is the front line in an ongoing struggle to control the ways in which people choose to access media. Such battles are not new. In the 1980s a similar battle was fought between the competing formats in the video age, for example, VHS vs. BetaMax. Sony originally had 100% of the video market with BetaMax and the challenger for the title was JVC's VHS. Popular myth has it that BetaMax was technically superior but VHS had twice the capacity of Sony's hour-long tapes.[1] Battle commenced, but by 1988 Sony conceded and started to produce VHS video players themselves.

The outcome of this conflict was decided by the interaction of a number of factors: price, convenience, availability and technology. Today we see history repeating itself but with important variations. The outcome of this battle is all the more important as it will have a huge impact on not only the world of web filmmaking but on the whole of the media. We should note that this is a fast moving war and the situation changes rapidly. In early 2004, however, the battle lines are being drawn between software giants Microsoft, Apple, online digital media corporation, RealNetworks and the Open Source movement along with a few others, and this war will ultimately decide how audiences will consume their media. The central question to our examination is this: why is there a battle to control media formats?

Media Battles

In simple terms, the reason why any of these groups may wish to control the media format is because controlling the format means money. Each time a person wishes to watch a video, listen to a song or even play a game over the internet they will generally use a piece of software known as a 'media player'. It is the aim of each company concerned to be the media player of choice, every time. This would give the company direct access to the consumer in terms of subscriptions, advertising, selling CDs and so forth. The potential revenue is enormous. For example RealNetworks received $46.9 million in revenue from the quarter ended March 31st 2003, purely in sales in online media.[2] In addition, that quarter saw RealNetworks trumpeting their millionth paid subscriber. As wireless and internet technologies begin to deliver content to an ever-increasing audience, the importance of this market will grow, with new media companies such as RealNetworks vying alongside the BBC for domination.[3]

Common Standards

The internet has a set of common standards for webpages, known as Hyper Text Mark-up Language or HTML. A basic instruction in HTML to display some text in bold might look like this: <B>Display in Bold</B> – see Appendix VI.

```
table border="0" width="100%" cellspacing="0" cellpadding="0">
tr> <!-- Main table with navigation on the left -->
td width="137" valign="top" background="images/reduced_images/tv
table border="0" cellspacing="0" cellpadding="0" height="100%">
tr valign="top" background="../images/reduced_images/tv_left_str
td width="137" height="100%"> <img border="0" src="images/reduce
area coords="17,252,107,275" href="http://www.plugincinema.com/p
area coords="17,228,104,252" href="http://www.plugincinema.com/p
area coords="17,205,105,228" href="http://www.plugincinema.com/p
area coords="17,137,106,161" href="http://www.plugincinema.com/p
area coords="18,115,106,137" href="http://www.plugincinema.com/p
area coords="18,94,106,115" href="http://www.plugincinema.com/pl
area coords="18,73,107,94" href="http://www.plugincinema.com/plu
```

A sample of the HTML that powers plugincinema!

Using HTML means that the information on the internet is accessible regardless of the operating system used, such as Apple OS, Windows, Unix or Linux. This is because the information conforms to set standards being used to send or receive the data. These standards are maintained by an organisation known as the World Wide Web Consortium. While users may choose different web browsers to view their webpages (such as Microsoft Explorer, Netscape Navigator, Opera or Mozilla) they will all see the same information. (This is not the entire story – however, the issues surrounding browser compatibility would fill another book!) The problem comes when one organisation or company decides to depart from the standard; it threatens the interconnectedness and therefore the functioning of the entire internet. With such dire consequences, why then would anyone want to break the standard? The answer is that there is a considerable amount of money to be made from the browser, internet development tools and web server markets. Companies try to introduce new features to set their products apart from the competition. These often vary from the multi-compatible standards agreed upon. Thus, there is a strained dynamic between compatibility and proprietary technology.

The Video Dynamic

The issue of standardisation gets more complex with audio and video as the volume and complexity of the data grows. The first standards were originally moderated by a loose group of interested parties known as the Moving Pictures Experts Group and were so referred to as MPEG, with a numerical suffix (The MPEG name coming from the group assigned the task of developing these standards). The Moving Pictures Experts Group is now a sub group of ISO/IEC (International Organization for Standardization/International Electrotechnical Commission). From here came MPEG-1, the optimised media format for CD-ROMs and subsequently MPEG-2, which has been adopted as the standard used for digital TV. This development of standards is an ongoing process and continues to this day, but those currently under development include: 'MPEG-4, as a standard for next generation video delivered over the internet and MPEG-7, as the standard for describing and searching for audio and visual content.'[4] MPEG-4 is, therefore, the standard that is of interest to filmmakers on the internet. This standard aims at determining how the bitstream operates but not the Codec (compression/ decompression tool). In other words, it is the standard that defines how the audio/video data should be 'bundled' for passage over the internet (the bitstream) but leaves the process of bundling up the data in order to send, and the reassembling of the data when it arrives (the Codec) as an open area. As such, a common standard is available for sending the data, but the various companies making software are free to innovate in terms of the development of better Codecs.

The Moving Pictures Experts Group can develop new MPEG standards for the internet or indeed any other technology, however, persuading software companies to adopt them in the file format wars, is another matter altogether. This is more an issue of inter-company politics and commercial manoeuvring. A major current combatant is the ISMA (Internet Streaming Media Alliance), a trade group with members such as Apple Computers, Cisco Systems and Sun Microsystems, which is pushing for the adoption of open standards and intellectual property protection on behalf of the industry. Invited to join, but absent from the ISMA are the two media heavyweights Microsoft and RealNetworks. All of the big internet video companies such as Apple, Microsoft and RealNetworks have their flirtations and disagreements with the MPEG standards. (For example Apple currently support MPEG-4 but have had license disagreements, RealNetworks are compatible with it but still maintain their distance and Microsoft have not accepted it as a standard.) All of which illustrates the current fractured nature of the standards debate.

Reports from the Front Line

So who is winning the war? Realistically it is very difficult to be sure and for the reasons discussed below, almost pointless to speculate. It is difficult to say because the gathering of accurate statistics is a complex task. There have been frequent upsets in this area, for example, Apple's 2002 highly publicised criticism of research group Nielsen/NetRatings' methodology led to a change in research methods and a new report. It could also be that speculation is pointless since many users simply install multiple media players and adopt usage patterns that are often erratic and vary upon the media being consumed. To further confuse the area new factors come into play quickly and often without any warning. The short and bountiful history of the internet is so convoluted it can change seemingly overnight. One such example would be the arrival of media player DivX in 1999 – it has gained ground rapidly, claiming over 30 million users by July 2003,[5] compared to Apple's 100 million users and RealNetworks 270 million (figures from June 2002[6]) (see Chapter 1). DivX gained its notoriety and arguably its users, not so much from the streaming of media but more from the file trading movies over the internet.

As Microsoft's deal with Time Warner in 2003 shows – alliances can also be used to capture new markets and rapidly change the battle lines.[7] With the largest software company in the world joining forces with the largest entertainment company in the world, would this meeting of giants strike the winning blow in the file trade wars? Maybe not. RealNetworks has shown that the front line extends beyond existing media networks by clinching a deal with major European mobile phone networks to supply software for what is arguably the next generation of media devices.[8] Apple has had their significant victories also. The QuickTime format is used on the Apple Movie Trailers website, a hugely popular resource where people can view the latest trailers for many Hollywood movies. Apple also presided over the launch of the iTunes service[9], where media files (in this case audio MP3s) can be paid for and downloaded over the internet. While not unique in this service, Apple's experience and proprietary hardware paid off with a million songs being downloaded in just the first week of trading.[10]

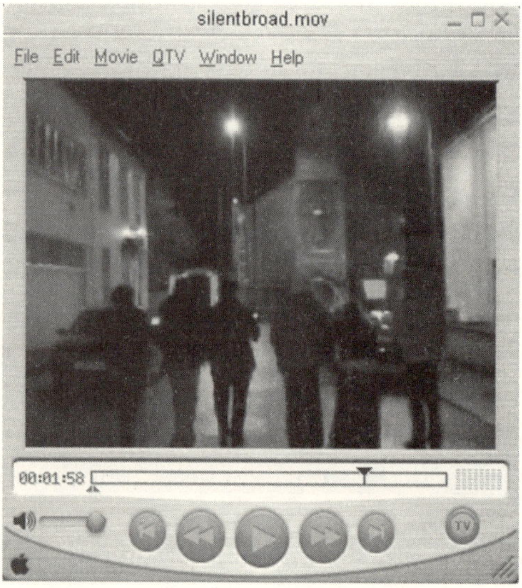

***Silent Night*, plugincinema.com, 2002 (QuickTime)**

There are also other companies besides these three 'giants' making media players, the Open Source movement, for example, is gaining ground rapidly. Take the example of MPlayer[11]– an Open Source player that the developers claim can handle MPEG 1, 2 and 4 as well as some RealNetworks and Windows Media files. There is also the popular Winamp Media Player, estimated to be in use by well over 15 million people worldwide.[12] So the battle continues…

Free Players

While all the major companies in the battle offer a very basic media player, at no cost, the free software advocate Richard Stallman is critical of the very un-free nature of the technology that powers such software: 'Most of these are released using secret proprietary standards and free software cannot access them. In most cases, we cannot write the free software because the format is secret. In the US and Europe, such free software is illegal when it does exist.' For those who wish to adhere to the philosophy of the Free Software Movement and support a decentralised film movement (see Chapter 3), this is a serious issue, as Richard goes on to explain, 'For those of us who want to maintain our freedom and our control over our computers, all this music and video is simply unavailable. We cannot access it at all.' There are still other options available however – filmmakers can distribute their work using older, more accessible technology, such as MPEG1 and using methods other than streaming (see Chapter 11).[13]

Why does it Matter?

A filmmaker needs to be in touch, if only loosely, with the ebb and flow of the file format wars. The outcome of this battle will have a direct effect upon the filmmaking process (see Chapter 10) and the technology chosen to distribute the work (see Chapter 11). Even before you have made a film, the question of the file format can have a direct impact on the methods of production that are chosen, for example, it would be no use planning a film with fast action and cutting without considering the impact of your chosen file format.

During the battle for supremacy with VHS vs. Betamax, most people occupied the position of consumer, and the primary concern for rival companies was to persuade consumers to buy their technology. However as a filmmaker you are now both a consumer and a producer of films; you are not just an observer of the ongoing battle but a participant, whether willing or not. It is therefore vital that you, as a filmmaker, are well-informed and able to make judgements on what is best for your work and your audience.

Links for Further Thinking

Apple Trailers
http://www.apple.com/trailers

Apple's QuickTime
http://www.apple.com/quicktime

DivX
http://www.divx.com

Free Codecs – Independent versions of mainstream codecs
http://www.freecodecs.com

Internet Streaming Media Alliance
http://www.isma.tv/home

Microsoft's Windows Media Player
http://www.microsoft.com/windows/windowsmedia

Moving Pictures Experts Group Homepage
http://www.chiariglione.org/mpeg/index.htm

MPEG 2 FAQ
http://bmrc.berkeley.edu/frame/research/mpeg/mpeg2faq.html

MPlayer
http://www.mplayerhq.hu/homepage/design6/info.html

Nullsoft's Winamp Media Player
www.winamp.com

RealNetworks
http://www.real.com

Wide Web Consortium
http://www.w3.org/World

References and Notes

1 Helge Moulding's email to alt.folklore.urban contains a full description of the VHS/Betamax story.
http://www.urbanlegends.com/products/beta_vs_vhs.html

2 Source was RealNetworks press release, April 29th 2003.
http://www.realnetworks.com/company/press/releases/2003/q103results.html

3 For an example read 'RealNetworks Partners With BBC, among others' on ASPnews.com.
http://www.aspnews.com/news/article.php/2178741

4 For more info see the Moving Picture Experts Group's website.
http://www.chiariglione.org/mpeg/index.htm

5 Source was DivX Networks press release, January 31th 2002.
www.divxnetworks.com/press/pr_detail.php?pr_id=15

6 Source was a ZDnet article, June 19th 2002.
http://zdnet.com.com/2102-1105_2-937379.html

7 For full on the deal see
http://zdnet.com.com/2100-1107_2-1012512.html

8 For full on the deal see
http://www.computerweekly.com/Article122725.htm

9 See the iTunes website for more information.
http://www.apple.com/music

10 This figure was quoted by a CNet article.
http://news.com.com/2100-1027_3-999701.html

11 See the MPlayer website for more information.
http://www.mplayerhq.hu/homepage/design6/news.html

12 Figures quoted by iBroadcast.com in article Sep 16th 1999.
http://www.ibroadcast.com/site/technology/mp3.shtml

13 There is a plugincinema article on approaches to 'lo-fi' technology http://www.plugincinema.com/plugin/articles/lofi.htm and for more on Richard Stallman see http://www.stallman.org

Chapter 3: The Rights and Wrongs of Copyright

Nailing Down Copyright

Copyright aims to place fixed legal boundaries around what are essentially ethereal thoughts. However, attempting to define the creative process is always difficult and inevitably involves a subjective judgement. For example, the Texas Tech University School of Art Copyright Guidelines note that to be a unique creation, a work must be, '...the result of original independent authorship (the entire work does not have to be original. It can be based on prior copyrighted or non-copyrighted material),' and there must be, '...a minimal element of creativity present.'[1] If a dispute about copyright arises, then some authority must be called upon to make the judgment as to the originality and level of creativity present.

At first sight it may appear that copyright is a done deal: if you make a film, it is yours and you control it. The Motion Picture Association of America's site, respectcopyrights.org, espouses this opinion: 'Copyright is a form of legal protection provided to the authors of creative works. The purpose of copyright is to encourage the creation of educational, entertaining and aesthetically pleasing works that enrich society.'[2] But as any artist knows, creativity has always been built upon and enriched by what has gone before. Given that art relies on an evolution and maturation of ideas from previous forms, it is clear that the boundaries of artistic provenance are blurry at best. An illustration of this is the controversy surrounding the cult 1992 film *Reservoir Dogs* by director Quentin Tarantino. As the film gained in cult status, a trail of reports pointed to the marked similarities between it and an earlier Hong Kong movie, *City On Fire*, directed by Ringo Lam. Both films concerned a heist gone wrong and it was alleged that the plot, and many of the scene compositions, had been copied. Indeed one filmmaker, Mike White, edited a montage of footage from the two films called

Who Do You Think You Are Fooling? (WDYTYF) to point to what he saw as the marked similarities that Tarantino had never owned up to, 'I thought *Reservoir Dogs* was a total flash of brilliance... To see it had been taken from something else, I felt kind of cheated.'[3]

White's film was accepted into the 1995 New York Underground Film Festival, but was pulled out of a press screening, reportedly due to pressure from sensitive parties.[4] The festival director at the time and the distributors of *Reservoir Dogs*, Miramax, both denied that pressure was brought to bear in removing the film. White later commented that: 'There's the idea that a festival showing WDYTYF was threatened by Miramax that the fest organizers needed "clip licenses". Meanwhile, there are others who would consider WDYTYF well within the doctrines of fair use as they view it more as "news" than entertainment. From what I understand, news channels don't need to acquire "clip licenses" when using footage during a news story. Copyright is all too fluid at times.'[5] Indeed, in the current structure of copyright, the definition of where the border lies is a legal one and therefore one that a filmmaker must learn to recognise. Whether one chooses to respect the borders is ultimately a personal choice, but it is worth bearing in mind what the consequences of crossing these borders might be.

This may seem to over-complicate what ought to be an essentially simple issue: you make a film and copyright law ensures that it is protected. This is certainly the way the mainstream film industry works; the profit a film derives is from the sales of physical reproductions of the original (i.e. cinema film prints, DVD and VHS/PAL video). This practice is quite different on the internet, however, as most things are. As discussed in Chapter 1, in this arena at least, the concept of copyright is indeed under threat. When using the internet as a means through which to distribute their work, an artist needs to consider the range of approaches available to them. In essence, there are three broad categories of copyright protection that a filmmaker can consider using: copyright, copyleft and anticopyright.

Defining Copyright

To follow the mainstream route and respect traditional boundaries is to enter the realm of copyright. Regardless of whether you consciously aim to copyright your work or not, in most countries your work will be copyrighted as a matter of course. The very act of creation is enough to gain the protection of the law. A good example is provided by the UK law:

> You do not need to register copyright – there is no official registration system. This is why protection is said to be automatic. So long as you have created a work that qualifies for copyright protection, that is, it falls into one of the categories of material protected by copyright, then you will have copyright protection without having to do anything to establish this.[6]

Indeed, most international conventions stipulate that copyright is automatic and not dependent on registration. What the law states cannot be copyrighted are more ethereal things such as ideas: 'Although the work itself may be protected, the idea behind it is not.' [7] So, Ringo Lam's ideas in *City on Fire* being 'borrowed' by Tarantino does not appear to breach legal boundaries in the UK – or does it? The law does have something to say on plagiarism: 'It is important to remember that if you copy less than the whole of a copyright work thinking that you are only copying the idea behind it, you may actually be copying a substantial part of the copyright work.'[8] So who has the last word? 'For some copyright works people say that it is the expression of an idea that has copyright protection rather then the underlying idea. However, the borderline between expression and idea is very difficult to define – ultimately only the courts can do this."[9] For *City on Fire*, as neither party ever chose to test the alleged plagiarism in the courts, it was never legally tested.

This highlights an important point; you may consider that a piece of work is original and is yours, but if you believe you have been the subject of a copyright infringement, then the courts are the only place to establish whether or not your claim can be upheld. While this is no problem to a large multinational media company with deep pockets, for individual filmmakers it could be a problem.

Urban myth suggests that to ensure that your ideas are protected, all you need to do is post your script/treatment/film in an envelope back to yourself. The idea is that once the post-marked envelope arrives back on your doorstep you are reputedly safe. However, this is not the case. Anyone wishing to play devil's advocate could argue that you have simply mailed an empty envelope to yourself, which you filled with the copyrighted material at a later date. Alternatively, some suggest putting a copy of your work into the vault of your local bank, which can be a surprisingly cheap way of date-stamping your work. Still others have suggested placing a copy with the family solicitor or lawyer for safekeeping. Either way, if you think your work is in danger of predation, you will need to take proper advice to establish your legal position since the courts will be the final arbitrators.

Sticking to the traditional approach is free and easy to do (as it is automatic, see above) and will ensure that you retain absolute control over your work. However, if you are worried about your work being copied, then enforcing your free copyright protection is another matter altogether. The decision rests with the law in your country of residence. It is also possible that in the digital realm you are limiting the spread of your work, as the fences that protect it may also serve to keep interested people out.

Copyleft

In the words of author and copyleft advocate Michael Stutz copyleft is defined as: '...a way to license a work so that unrestricted redistribution, copying and modification is permitted, provided that all copies and derivatives retain the exact same licensing.'[10] At first glance this might seem like a contradictory statement – offering both the right to unrestricted redistribution but with restrictions. However, this is not the case; it only offers people the right to freely copy the work provided they do not break the rules under which that right is granted. The ideas of copyleft are synonymous with the concept of 'Open Source' and the 'Free Software Movement', though these latter terms are related to software code and development. Michael Stutz, author of the Linux Cookbook, believes the origin of the idea comes from the very nature of the digital networks that now span the world. In a recent interview he stated, 'The idea of copyleft is that suddenly, with computer networks and digital files, it becomes painless to make any number of copies of a work. Whereas with film, if I had a 35mm film for instance and I wanted to share it with you, I'd have to lend you my physical copy. With computer networks, that has changed – the work is no longer bound to a particular physical object, but is merely a file, that we can copy as many times as we like.'[11]

Copyleft ideas evolved from the Open Source movement, whose core principles dictate that software developers make the 'source files' they use to construct software freely available. By providing these source files it becomes possible for others to see what makes the software tick and enables them to modify it for their own needs. Which in turn, leads to improvements in the original source code, enabling it to evolve. The Open Source movement has its roots in the ideas of the Free Software Movement, although their particular ideological stances differ.[12]

The copyleft license that covers the public releases of code ensures that anyone modifying or passing on the information, in any form, is not profiting from or restricting the original work. This is a radical departure from the commodity based economic system that has traditionally been used. Michael Stutz argues that these new copyleft systems are still economically viable. As he states, 'The idea of copyleft is that its much more profitable for a publisher if a work is accessible from anywhere via the internet, free for anyone to share (as with Linux). The authors and publishers can still make money, of course – in fact, I believe with music and other forms of works, copyleft can make the publishers more money than the traditional ways. You don't make the money selling the computer file but you sell a larger distribution containing sources (with music, for instance, publishers of copylefted albums sell them on DVD).'[13] Certainly the upward sales of DVDs, bolstered by extras such as director's commentaries and deleted scenes, which are arguably the film equivalent of the 'source files', seem to back up the case being made. In the US there was a 57% increase in DVD sales in the first quarter of 2003 alone![14] Another good example of this is RedHat, the Linux company that makes some of its money from the distribution of Linux but not from the copyright of Linux itself. RedHat are proud of this model, stating on their website that, 'The Open Source model is built not on the power to lock-in customers, but consistently serving them through extraordinary value, flexibility and ease of integration and management... It's a fundamental change and its working. We are profitable, have $287 million in the bank and have close productive partnerships with the top names in our industry, Dell, HP, IBM, Intel, Oracle. Our business is solid and self-sufficient.'[15]

Releasing your work into the public realm as copyleft certainly offers filmmakers a realistic method of addressing the issues created when using the internet as a distribution method. The copyleft status of your work will encourage others to use and modify your work and therefore promote it; often to a far greater degree than you could have achieved on your own. This may lead to you being unable to profit from the traditional methods of copyright but it will also limit anyone else; the copyleft status of your work means there is no profit to be made by less scrupulous people in adopting your work as their own. You do, of course, also have to be prepared to let go of your creation. Although, you could unwittingly find that you have contributed to create an even greater masterpiece.

Anticopyright

The exact method by which copyleft operates is still of concern to some commentators. They argue that the copyleft concept still requires a functioning and viable copyright system as a base. Lawyer Paul Lambert of LK Shields Solicitors told *Wired* magazine that, '...as a fundamental concept, copyright remains, because copyleft can't work without copyright.'[16]

By contrast to the two options so far discussed, anti-copyright is a rejection of any legal framework for ownership altogether. It is a total rejection of any borders or boundaries on creative ideas. Anticopyright takes the copyleft notion that creativity benefits from a lack of ownership and merges it with radical political ideas into a whole new concept. This concept arguably stems from a similar ideology to the statement, 'All property is theft', which was popularised by the French writer Pierre-Joseph Proudhon in the political writings he circulated in Paris in1840. Proudhon was reacting against what he saw as a fundamental inequality within the structure of the society in which he was living. He declared that, 'The right of property was the origin of evil on the earth, the first link in the long chain of crimes and misfortunes which the human race has endured since its birth.'[17]

For some sectors of digital culture the notion that the earth is a common treasury has become intertwined with ideas surrounding shared ownership. A representative of the online anarchist community infoshop.org expands these ideas as follows:

> ...that's one of our heartfelt beliefs. Free ideas and information benefit everyone, not just a few selfish individuals. Certainly making music more available increases creativity...piracy is part of the price they pay for their overpricing and monopoly.[18]

***Leave Me Alone*, Dir. Tomas Rawlings, 2000 (Flash)**

John Oswald summarised this up well with his well-known comment that, 'If creativity is the field, copyright is the fence.'[19] By abandoning the fences, a filmmaker can experiment and play with any idea or theme they desire; copyrighted media artefacts can be sampled and re-mixed, ideas can be plundered and reinvented. However, there is a flip side. Many filmmakers who choose this path retain a degree of anonymity to ensure that they are not pursued, as copyright law is still operating. Once created and released, the anticopyright filmmaker has no control over any of the original work, as its creation and distribution may have also have violated the laws of copyright.

The power of this idea is well-illustrated by the short film *Star Wars: Episode II Teaser Trailer*, by a filmmaker calling themselves the 'Anonymous Director'. This short film used copyrighted material from a variety of film sources including the *Star Wars* franchises, *Braveheart* and *Dune*.[20] The short film was posted on *Star Wars* fans sites and is estimated to have exceeded a million downloads.

Fan Warfare

By enforcing copyright, some intellectual property (IP) owners have found that they are biting the hand that feeds them. This is aptly demonstrated in the PotterWar saga. The owners of the *Harry Potter* license, Warner Brothers, decided that fan websites dedicated to the teenage wizard created by J K Rowling were in infringement of copyright. In December 2000 the Warner Brothers legal department promptly set about protecting their IP. To the dedicated young Hogwarts fans who were their targets, however, this was nothing short of war. PotterWar.org.uk was one of the sites which led the struggle to keep the fan sites up and running, and by March 2001 the fans declared victory. Warner Bros finally conceded, realising a little late maybe that it was the same fans who were the main consumers of *Harry Potter* merchandise.[21]

Harry Potter fans are not the only ones to experience the wrath of copyright holders. In June 2000 the fan club of a *Star Wars* character based at the website Bobbafett.com received a legal 'cease and desist' letter from the copyright owners, Lucasfilm Ltd.[22] Shortly afterwards however, it seems that Lucasfilm suffered a change of heart, as five months after this event the 'Bobba Fett' fan site is still up and running with no pending legal action. A Lucasfilm spokesperson commented on the situation in a Salon.com article, stating that provided the fans are not seeking commercial gain, they are free to use the copyrighted material with both an informal agreement and the blessing of George Lucas (the creator of *Star Wars*).[23]

For most content creators, in this post-modern age the plundering of cultural resources on the internet is practically a rite of passage; however, anyone wishing to use the net in this way should first consider their options carefully. So what is the best course of action if you wish to release either copyright or copyleft work that contains samples from other copyrighted material? This depends upon:

- **The IP you are choosing to work with** For example, if you are choosing to use the *Star Wars* IP, as has already been discussed, you will be able to work with it and distribute your work – provided you adhere to the guidelines the IP holder, Lucas film has set-up.[24]
- **Which elements of that IP you will be using** For example, if you wished to do a film based on the cult writings of HP Lovecraft, you'd need to be selective about which of his characters and places you choose to use. While some of his work, such as anything written before 1923, is now public domain and therefore out of copyright and ok to plunder, other aspects of his work have a legal status depending on whether the copyright was renewed or not (this covers works published from 1923 to 1963, whose copyright was not renewed in the US.)[25]
- **The prevailing attitude of the IP owner to existing fan works** For example, as discussed the *Harry Potter* IP holders are quite lenient towards fan works, though if you'd been working on a *Harry Potter* fan film prior to the battle documented in PotterWar.co.uk, then it might have been a different matter.[26]
- **Whether you are intending homage, parody or insults.** It is reasonable to expect that an IP owner, especiallly if you can contact them directly, might be more disposed to giving permission for work that is a

homage to their IP than a work that insults it. Their attitude may also depend on whether you intend to make money on the back of their work or not: is it a more experimental/community project than a directly commercial one?

- **The legal status of the country in which you are working** A good illustration of this is the graphic novel *The Wasteland* by Martin Rowson. This novel parodied elements of the poem of the same name by T.S.Eliot. The edition to be published in the UK went to great lengths to avoid possible legal action and so had to alter sections of the book to comply with the requests of T.S.Eliot's estate. By contrast, the US edition, under far less pressure thanks to the constitutionally protected right to free speech, was able to publish as the author intended.[27]

If you choose to stay within the laws of copyright, there is research to be done but with the many resources available to help you this shouldn't prove difficult.[28]

Copying the Future

The future of copyright, copyleft and anticopyright is being decided by battles currently taking place all over the globe. The front line troops for this war are the PCs of artists who are sampling from the cultural mainstream, as well as in the courtrooms and multinational corporations. Like millions of others to whom technology is a second language, Michael Shultz is also aware that we live in interesting times: 'We're currently in a transitional period, and the question remains the same as before: how to facilitate a shared commons, where publishers who wilfully participate may release work to their protection and potentially their profit, and in a way that the works can be shared and examined in full by anyone, so that civilization may progress.'

Links for Further Thinking

Anarchism
http://www.infoshop.org

Chilling Effect's 'Frequently Asked Questions about Fan Fiction'
http://www.chillingeffects.org/fanfic/faq.cgi

Copyleft
http://dsl.org/copyleft

Electronic Freedom Foundation's 'Fair Use FAQ'
http://www.eff.org/IP//eff_fair_use_faq.html

Mike White's Anti-Tarantino Page
http://www.impossiblefunky.com/qt

MPAA's Pro-copyright Site
http://www.respectcopyrights.org

Texas Tech University School of Art Copyright Guidelines
http://www.art.ttu.edu/artdept/copyright%20frameset/terms.html

UK Government IP Site
http://www.intellectual-property.gov.uk

Star Wars 'fake' Episode II Trailer
http://www.theforce.net/theater/trailers/episodeii/index.shtml

References and Notes

1 http://www.art.ttu.edu/artdept/copyright%20frameset/terms.html

2 http://www.respectcopyrights.org/whatiscopyright.html

3 http://www.impossiblefunky.com/qt/RD_1.html

4 See the clipping in the *New York Daily News* from 31st June 1995, archived on Michael's site.
http://www.impossiblefunky.com/qt/pdf/nydailynews.pdf

5 From an interview for this book dated 2003.

6 From the Government-backed website about UK intellectual

property on the internet.
http://www.intellectual-property.gov.uk/std/faq/copyright/auto_protection.htm

7 See above.
http://www.intellectual-property.gov.uk/std/faq/copyright/ideas.htm

8 See above.
http://www.intellectual-property.gov.uk/std/faq/copyright/ideas.htm

9 See above.
http://www.intellectual-property.gov.uk/std/faq/copyright/ideas.htm

10 From Michael Stutz's copyleft website. http://www.dsl.org/copyleft

11 http://www.plugincinema.com/plugin/articles/opensourcefilms.htm

12 The two approaches differ in ideology rather than methodology, and in the words of the founder of the FSF, Richard Stallman: 'The Free Software movement and the Open Source movement are like two political camps within the free software community.' From the article, 'Why Free Software is better than Open Source.'
http://www.gnu.org/philosophy/free-software-for-freedom.html

13 http://www.plugincinema.com/plugin/articles/opensourcefilms.htm

14 Figures from DVD Entertainment Group, an industry trade association, quoted in *The Arizona Republic.*
http://www.azcentral.com/arizonarepublic/business/articles/0804dvds04.html

15 http://www.redhat.com/about/mission/business_model.html

16 From the *Wired* article which stated that: 'If a creative work was of sufficient quality and uniqueness, "copyright manifests automatically," he said. "It's created by statute – you can't get away from that. Therefore, copyleft is not the end of copyright as we know it, as some critics have argued", he said. "Software developers can thus not disclaim copyright, but may either license or assign the work to others."'
http://www.wired.com/news/print/0,1294,41679,00.html

17 http://dhm.best.vwh.net/archives/proudhon-ch3.html

18 From an interview conducted for this book in 2003.

19 A commonly used quote, we found it here: http://www.plunderphonics.com

20 A full account of this can be found on CNN: http://www.cnn.com/2000/TECH/computing/08/11/fake.starwars

21 A full account of this can be found on PotterWar.org.uk: http://www.potterwar.org.uk/history.html

22 See Lucas Films June 15th 2000 letter. http://www.bobafettfanclub.com/lucasfilm.shtml

23 http://archive.salon.com/tech/feature/2000/11/16/fan_films/print.html

24 You can read more about this and how to enter the *Star Wars* Fan Film competitions at http://atomfilms.shockwave.com/af/spotlight/collections/starwars

25 "The oldest and strongest emotion of mankind is fear, and the oldest and strongest kind of fear is fear of the unknown," Lovecraft, 1927. See http://quote.wikipedia.org/wiki/Howard_Phillips_Lovecraft
There is a discussion on copyright of written work on Slashdot at http://yro.slashdot.org/yro/02/10/23/1651238.shtml and you can also see a discussion of Lovecraft's work at http://www.kuro5hin.org/story/2003/9/1/172415/6523

26 Once again see http://www.potterwar.org.uk

27 http://www.cinemagebooks.com/si/006195.html

28 For more information see the article 'FanFiction: Fan's Right or Copyright Nightmare?' http://www.kuro5hin.org/story/2003/7/18/175640/391

Chapter 4: Business at the Speed of Light

The Prequel

This chapter discusses the possible avenues a web filmmaker can explore to turn talent into an income. Before we delve further into this area, however, it is worth taking a step back and asking: what advantages are there to striking out into the uncharted territory that is web filmmaking? Why, given the uncertainties and the huge amount of work it would entail, would anyone be interested in attempting to travel this path? Why not pursue more traditional avenues, seeking a job in television or at a Hollywood film studio for example?

To begin with, it will come as no surprise to learn that getting work in the traditional film and TV industry is also full of uncertainties and hard work. The advice given by film-tv.co.uk, is typical of that offered to those seeking fame and fortune in this area: 'The media industry is a tough business and getting that foot in the door is only achieved by sheer hard work and persistence.'[1] In 2002, plugincinema spoke at the UK based 9th Sheffield International Documentary Festival,[2] alongside representatives from Discovery Channel and Channel 4. Both representatives from the television industries echoed this position. The advice given by film-tv.co.uk to those wishing to make their own films using traditional media structures is equally as bleak: 'How many [films] folded during production? Find out how many were released, how many were released and disappeared without trace within a week, how many went straight to video, how many have made any money, how many production companies were formed and went to the wall within a year… Be realistic, the chances of success are very slim.'

It is reasonable, therefore, to suggest that it is as difficult to make it within traditional media structures, as it is in web filmmaking. If there is indeed such a thing as parity, in terms of difficulty, then why not consider web filmmaking? The main difficulty for web films lies in the fact that as the medium is so new there are no previously trodden paths to use for guidance. This is also their lure! Those who take to the waters of web filmmaking are the pioneers of not only new technologies, but of new ways of organising an entire new industry.

If nothing else, developing your web filmmaking ability will enhance your understanding of emerging technologies, whilst equipping you with a useful set of new skills. Indeed, there are various examples of filmmakers whose online exploits have brought them to the attention of Hollywood. Once such duo is Bruce Branit and Jeremy Hunt. In 2000 the two made a short film entitled *405 The Movie* (as mentioned in the introduction) which depicts a DC-10 aircraft landing on an LA freeway. *Wired* reported in August 2000 that, following huge attention and accolade focused on the film, the two were signed to Creative Artists Agency, who have a reputation of being one of the top talent agencies in Hollywood.[3]

New Realities

Changes in technology can create commercial successes and failures, often within a very short period of time. The impact of internet technology on the media has been massive and is on-going. The technology commentator, Ben 'Mouse' McShane, writing in *The Ball State Daily News*, predicated a harsh reality for one particular arm of the media, the music industry:

> I don't dispute that a recorded song is intellectual property. I don't dispute that file-sharing is theft. I dispute the idea that it can be regulated, let alone stopped... The truth is they will never stop us from stealing music off of the internet. We have tasted the fruit and we find it quite delectable.[4]

Are we, as discussed in Chapter 1, in fact witnessing the beginning of the end of copyright? Will the 21st century reveal that the established practices of the vertically integrated media production conglomerates can no longer work? It is true that the music industry's sales worldwide are still in decline[5], and as a response the principal industry body, the US based Recording Industry Association of America (RIAA), is pursuing anti-piracy actions in an attempt to stem the flow of file traded music. The harsh reality of the situation is backed-up by research from OC&C Strategy Consultants in a report filed in February 2002. This report concluded that the fight against music piracy had already been lost and that films and games are the next battleground. One of the report's authors, Sarah Davison, made a notable remark about what some see as the reality of the situation: 'It may not be too late for entertainment industries to turn this around, but [there's] not as much time as executives seem to think.'[6]

This statement was aimed at the 'entertainment industries'. If this is the possible shape of things to come, how will filmmakers be able to ply their trade in a world without copyright? Even if the predictions prove overly pessimistic, what hope is there for filmmakers who need to make a living from their craft? The truth is that there is no established business model to look to. There are, however, companies and individuals already making a profit in this sector, and an increasing number of avenues opening up. It is a future that holds both uncertainty and opportunity.

Multi-skilled filmmaking

As you might have gathered from the book so far, the web filmmaker is a multi-skilled beast! However, creative talent and production skills alone are unlikely to make you a living in web filmmaking. In this highly competitive industry business skills are paramount to a production's success and an awareness of how to successfully handle administration, marketing, promotion and accounting is vital. These are the nuts and bolts of any commercial operation and their importance cannot be underestimated.

Operational Models

So what possible models of operation are available to the author of the new media businesses? In this chapter we will examine several emerging models. As with any branch of media and business there is no easy formula for commercial success – hard work, trial and error are part of the course. Fortunately there are some pioneers out there charting new territories, whose successes and failures are a source of valuable information to other potential web filmmakers planning a route into the wilds.

Subscription

There are now a considerable number of online companies who make money from a subscription-based model. One example is RealNetworks, a company that may be familiar to many internet users as the providers of the popular Real player streaming and media software (see Chapter 2). They also operate subscription-based media services, indeed, a CNet article of April 2002[7] noted that RealNetworks seems to be refocusing its attention less at the software area and more towards their subscription-based services offering 'content for cash'. It would be reasonable to speculate that this is because RealNetworks is making an increasing amount of money in this area. RealNetworks sales figures from the third quarter of 2002 reported that revenue from the subscription-based services was $28.2 million, a figure up $16 million from the same period in 2001.

RealNetworks' subscription offers paying customers a

large array of general and specialist content such as access to iFilm (the short film website), footage of European football's UEFA competition and specialist news services such as CNN's Sci-Tech channel. Other web companies, it seems, are not far behind. Yahoo announced in February 2003[8] that it too would launch a 'Platinum Yahoo' service and began the hunt for partners. In early September 2003 Yahoo announced a deal with British Telecom, which included broadband media content such as pop videos.[9] Even cult filmmaker David Lynch declared that TV is dead and subscription models are the future![10]

It is perfectly possible to set up your own subscription website and there are a number of tools that will help you do this[11]. You will need a website, a server to host your content, a membership system and a method of payment. It is suggested that you first read Chapter 11, which will provide the information you need about servers and hosting. From here try Appendix VI and write a webpage using HTML. There are a number of software packages you can purchase to set up and manage subscription systems such as aMember.[12]

RealNetworks' success seems to come from the fact that it offers people a mixture of very open content from general sites that would appeal to a mass-audience, but (in the main) also offers more specialised content such as news and sport. It can (using streaming technology) offer a huge array of channels and content. This is available to the viewer at his or her convenience and at a lower distribution cost than even a TV cable company is able to match. RealNetworks has also worked hard to secure deals with media companies and other websites such as the BBC, CNN and iFilm. What lessons can be drawn from this? With its mass-audience infrastructure, television cannot provide the specialist content of the internet. The expansion of successful subscription models means that there is now a need for exciting new content.

Fairshare

The concept of 'Fairshare' is the latest incarnation of a familiar concept combining donations and investments. It was set up by Ian Clarke, Steven Starr and Rob Kramer and came about as a, '...response to the impossibility of enforcing copyright law without restricting people's ability to communicate.'[13] It can be summed up as a scheme where the fans of an artist (musician, filmmaker, writer etc.) invest money in the artist themselves with the aim of both supporting the work they admire and profiting from any future success of the artist. Clarke, Starr and Kramer argue that this is a similar model to that used by mainstream creative businesses, which invest in a director or band with the hope of a return, only through this method the process is democratized. While at first glance this may sound like an impossible utopian vision, it is already a reality: in 2001 the UK Band Dodgy raised enough money to finance an album through this very method. The group raised £15,000 ($25,000) through internet based micro-payment systems (such as PayPal), combined with an appeal to their fan base. Fans were offered either a small share for £25 ($40), which also gave them a mention on the album sleeve, or a large share for £1000 ($1800) with a percentage of the profits from the sale of the album. Triumphantly, the band's website proclaimed '...we finally raised the entire recording budget to record their fourth and best album to date by encouraging fans, supporters and visitors to this marvellous site to "invest" in the album.'[14] If this has worked for music, it seems logical that the same ideology could be applied to other artistic outlets including online film.

This approach is echoed by free software advocate Richard Stallman, who asks, 'Can filmmakers make money from online viewers while respecting their freedom? One way is through voluntary contribution from fans which will be, in the long term, the best model. If the music player displays a box saying, "Click here to send one dollar to the band," many people in the developed world will occasionally send one. If they don't do it often enough, the government can run a PR campaign urging people to support their favourite bands this way. Instead of going against human nature by saying, "Stop sharing, sharing is evil, sharing is the moral equivalent of attacking a ship and killing the crew," this would say "Share music, but send a dollar to the band now and then."'

The exact method of organising a Fairshare scheme is down to the individual. However, the ones discussed have a few defining features that are worth considering. Firstly, they appeal to interested parties (such as a band's fan-base). Secondly, unlike traditional share schemes as found on the stock exchange, they do not promise anything financial in return for the contribution. They may offer other incentives (such as a mention in the sleeve notes of the CD) but the main reward comes from being involved in the production of a creative endeavour. Finally, they use the internet as an organising platform. It would be possible to organise such a venture using pre-internet communications technology, but by taking advantage of the internet, by having email lists, websites and such like, the administrative burden is lowered and the overall cost will also be reduced. One particularly vital tool now available is the technology to collect donations or payments over the internet. With all the advances in secure payment technology, collecting money, especially small amounts of money, is also a relatively straightforward thing to set up. There are a number of systems that can be used such as PayPal, Escrow or Network for Good.[15] There is a sample tutorial on using the PayPal system in Appendix VII.

Advertising

Of course, paid advertising powers much of our media, especially TV, where the promise of reaching a huge audience means companies will pay thousands to place adverts and sponsor shows. As such, it is no surprise that this method of generating revenue is in place within the arena of web films as well. This more traditional model can be seen in operation on websites such as AtomFilms, the short film site now owned by software company Macromedia. AtomFilms started showing adverts in late 2001[16] and other big-name film sites such as iFilm have also begun to follow suit.

In an adaptation of this method, some websites offer users the choice of viewing the content for free but having to watch an advert also, or paying a small fee and viewing it advert-free. To date the most notable users of this method are the online magazine Salon.com and the massively popular technical site Slashdot.org. Although both are text-based publications, there is no reason why this idea could not be adapted by enterprising filmmakers wishing to generate revenue.

Another method of advertisement-funded filmmaking with a twist came to light in March 2003. The digital broadcaster Pseudo announced plans for a one-hour show on hip-hop and rap culture entitled *One Nation* and hosted by rapper Ice-T[17]. A sponsor was lined up and a buzz generated. So far it sounded like a normal TV show and it was, except for one crucial aspect: it was not to be aired on TV. The show was to be distributed though the Kazaa file trade network. In this case, the more the show is copied, the more 'viewers' it gets and the more people see the sponsors' message: TV on your PC.

There are various different ways of organising advertising on a website. If you believe that people will want to pay to advertise on your site the simplest thing to do is to invite users to contact you. You can then discuss the style of advert and fee with them directly. Alternatively, you may prefer to use more sophisticated payment systems such as PayPal to administer transactions, and pieces of software such as EasyBanners or Ban Man Pro to manage the display of adverts.[18] Such software tools typically control which banners will be displayed and how many times each banner is displayed. The final option is to allow another company to manage the advertising on your site. This may well involve signing up to a banner advertising company such as Burst Media or DoubleClick.[19] These companies will ask you to place HTML code within your website that enables them to control the adverts that come to your site. An example of an independent website using advertising is Talking Points Memo, a weblog. An example of a banner ad system used and controlled by the website owner can be found at dSWAT.net, while an example of a website using a banner advert company to organise the advertising can be found at Box Office Mojo.[20.]

Commerce

Some film sites use the tried and tested method of experimenting with sales to ensure that they have a viable business model. This can involve something as simple as selling the relevant films on video or DVD, selling film-related merchandise or even selling the programs themselves to other broadcasters. Filmmakers can also use their film sites as places where they can sell their own filmmaking talents with the films becoming, in effect, giant advertisements for the talents of those involved.

A good example of this method in practice is Guerrilla News Network (GNN). The site is a highly politicised and articulate film/news/chat/ideas portal and the huge numbers of people visiting the site are not just attracted by the films, but also by the other resources the site offers. Arguably, this type of overt political filmmaking would find few takers in the mainstream TV and film world, yet the films made by GNN have obviously struck a chord with a sizable audience. Their documentary entitled *Crack the CIA* won the Audience Award at the 2002 Sundance Online Film Festival. In an interview for plugincinema, GNN's creative director Stephen Marshall is not shy to point out the reasoning behind the sites commercial tactics[21]: 'It is becoming increasingly evident that alternative/guerrilla filmmakers cannot depend on the mainstream media and their declining number of art house outposts to support their work, especially if they are challenging the core assumptions and foundations of the corporatist system. We just aren't compatible anymore.'

As a direct result of their 'anti-establishment' tactics, GNN was commissioned to make pop-videos for artists such as Dead Prez, Eminem and 50 Cent. Stephen Marshall notes, 'Independent mediaists have to engineer their own self-sufficient economic realities. We need to be serious about the business of sustaining our visions. In our case it is about selling our products to the critical mass who have assembled around our virtual hub. And tapping into the profits generated from our brand equity through directing music videos for major artists and record labels.'

The Future of Consumption

The future seems to herald the continuation of the consolidation within the mainstream media industries on a global scale. The media workers resource group 'Media Alliance' warned that such activity both damages job prospects and creativity[22]. One could argue that this stagnation is already taking hold, as reports surface that terrestrial broadcast industries are facing slumps in advertising revenue coupled with falling worldwide viewing figures. This trend was highlighted by the UK based Media Guardian of 7th February 2002, when they suggested that statistics were showing that: '...viewing has plummeted and crucial audiences, such as sixteen to thirty-four year-olds and high-earning ABC1s, are switching off in droves.'[23]

Hollywood also seems to be suffering from a form of self-imposed stagnation. The industry is blaming the failure in 2003 of several hyped cash-cows, such as *Charlie's Angles 2:*

Full Throttle, on new technology, such as mobile phones. Executives remarked that whilst the content of such 'summer' films is similar to that of previous years, the fact that audiences can text each other immediately to give their verdict, is killing box office returns.[24]

Richard Stallman, on the other hand, asks whether such changes are inherently bad: 'A producer told me that the publicity for a film typically costs more than making the film. All this waste could be avoided. The reduction in hype would be healthy for society and for the art of cinema... The common thread of all this is that I reject the assumption that a decrease in income for filmmakers is a disaster so great that it must be avoided no matter what the cost in freedom. It is not such a big deal, except in the minds of those who get rich from it now and want to continue. We should not cater to them.' Richard also suggests that one method of revenue generation in the digital age could be to levy a tax on computer connectivity services, which would then be distributed directly to artists whose work is distributed on these networks.[25]

Despite the highly publicised dot-com crash of 2000/1, there can be no doubt those opportunities within the non-mainstream media sectors are expanding. Usage of the internet continues to grow and as new technologies come on-stream there is an increasing array of media distribution models that go beyond existing methods.[26] Mobile phones have now reached the stage where, with certain limitations, short films can be viewed on their colour screens. This represents a new and emerging market ready to be tapped into by filmmakers who have cut their teeth working within the limitations of the internet and new media technologies.

Another example of new distribution practice came to fruition in Portland, USA. Coming almost full circle with a return to early film screenings, 'The Portable Cinema', which took advantage of the cheap and easy projector technology now available, toured the country showing independently made films.[27] The operator of the enterprise remarked, 'I want to help every filmmaker that submits a film. My profit will come from two places: the venue at which the showing is made and the personal enjoyment of experiencing the many films we show.'

In late 2003, a film entitled *This Is Not a Love Song*, written by the creator of *The Full Monty,* was premiered both in cinemas and online.[28] The film itself was shot using low cost digital cameras to keep the production costs low and the online version will be free for the first few thousand viewers whilst those following will pay only a nominal charge. This was a unique experiment in film exhibition, a mixture of real and online screenings with a financial model combining free views and subscription, ensuring that the next stage in the evolution of business at the speed of light is underway.

Perhaps the final words on this topic should be left to GNN's Stephen Marshall[29]: 'So what is happening is that a vacuum has opened up where there was once this vibrant competition between the dominant media houses. And there is suddenly room for a highly branded, charismatic and controversial set of challengers to take up the challenge and compete with the din and sparkle of the mainstream spectacle. But we have to come with our best stuff and not cry about being marginalized when we show Noam Chomsky at a podium in shaky MiniDV. You know? Now we have the tools and the techniques. They gave them to us. It's ours to lose. We have so much more vibrant creative energy within us and it is because we are on the outside and on the perimeter that we have the edge…Think Rome before the Fall.'

Links for Further Thinking

405 The Movie
http://www.405themovie.com

Atom Films
http://www.atomfilms.com

Dodgy
http://www.dodgy.co.uk

Fairshare
http://freenetproject.org/index.php?page=fairshare

Guerrilla News Network
http;//www.gnn.tv

Media Alliance
http://www.media-alliance.org

Pay Pal
http://www.paypal.com

Richard Stallman
http://www.stallman.org

salon.com
http://www.salon.com

This Is Not a Love Song
http://www.thisisnotalovesong.co.uk

References and Notes

1 http://www.film-tv.co.uk/frameset.asp?http://www.film-tv.co.uk/start/getting_a_job.asp

2 For a report on this event see http://www.plugincinema.com/plugin/articles/article_sidf2002.htm

3 http://www.wired.com/news/print/0,1294,38189,00.html

4 http://www.bsudailynews.com/vnews/display.v/ART/2003/07/03/3f046028dad40

5 http://news.com.com/2100-1023-883761.html

6 http://www.guardian.co.uk/Archive/Article/0,4273,4352035,00.html

7 http://news.com.com/2100-1023-878860.html

8 http://news.com.com/2100-1023-983894.html

9 http://www.netimperative.com/cmn/viewdoc.jsp?cat=all&docid=

BEP1_News_0000056842

10 'This is TV. This is the new television. And, you know, it's sort of absurd. They look as good on the internet as they would on TV. And why would you go over to TV? TV is dead.' http://www.streamingmedia.com/article.asp?id=8186

11 Try reading the article available at http://www.webpronews.com/ebusiness/smallbusiness/wpn20030821MakingMoneyfromaSubscriptionSite.html for a look at a few questions you might need to ask yourself.

12 For more on aMember see http://www.cgi central.net/scripts/amember This system is a good one for beginners as it is cheap and for an additional surcharge, the software company will install it and support you in running it.

13 http://freenetproject.org/index.php?page=fairshare

14 http://www.plugincinema.com/plugin/news/newslist2.php?keywrds=dodgy&Submit=Go

15 Fopr more on PayPal see Appendix VII or https://www.paypal.com and for more on Escrow see https://www.escrow.com and for more on Network for Good see http://www.networkforgood.org

16 http://news.com.com/2100-1023-271971.html

17 http://news.com.com/2100-1027-991396.html and http://www.rollingstone.com/news/newsarticle.asp?nid=17741

18 For more on Easy Banners see http://ebanners.escripts.net and for more on Ban Man Pro see http://www.banmanpro.com

19 For more on BustMedia see http://www.burstmedia.com and for more on DoubleClick see http://www.doubleclick.com Note that there is a useful information on possible banner ad companies at the website http://www.adbility.com

20 Talking Points Memo can be found at http://www.talkingpointsmemo.com while to see the dSWAT.net banner scroll to the bottom at http://www.dswat.net Note that this banner ad system is controlled by the shop software being used,

osCommerce. An example of a website using BurstMedia is Box Office Mojo at http://www.boxofficemojo.com

21 http://www.plugincinema.com/plugin/plugin_aesthetic/s_marshall.htm

22 The media activist song, 'Hymn of The Angels of The Public Interest' has the lrycis: 'You must protect the media made independently / Monopolies repress debate and creativity.' http://www.media-alliance.org/mediafile/22-1/dichter.html

23 The British Audience Research Board responded to this by pointing out that difficulties in data gathering were to blame for the low figures. The Media Guardian article also reported their concerns: '[The British Audience Research Board] said the data recorded when the old and new systems ran in parallel during December showed a "small overall audience drop" of 5%.' See http://media.guardian.co.uk/broadcast/story/0,7493,645925,00.html However, this decline has also been mirrored in Canadian figures '...the total average TV viewing hours of Canadians during the autumn of 1999 was 21.6 hours per week, a decrease of one hour from the previous year and even lower still than the previous minimum of 23.5 hours set in 1988.' (Figures quoted by NHK Broadcast Culture Research Institute.) See http://www.nhk.or.jp/bunken/media-diary-region/ur-r-2001-ame.html

24 For more information see http://news.independent.co.uk/digital/news/story.jsp?story=434778

25 Richard made this point in an interview for this book. It is an updated version of an earlier idea. See http://www.gnu.org/philosophy/dat.html

26 http://www.csmonitor.com/2001/1227/p13s1-stin.html

27 Reported in plugincinema news. http://www.plugincinema.com/plugin/newsarchive/news042001.htm

28 http://media.guardian.co.uk/mediaguardian/story/0,7558, 1028732,00.html

29 More from plugincinema's interview with Stephen: http://www.plugincinema.com/plugin/plugin_aesthetic/s_marshall.htm

Chapter 5: The pluginmanifesto

What is the pluginmanifesto?

> First came the Dogme 95 manifesto, where a collective of film directors founded in Copenhagen in spring 1995 expressed the goal of countering "certain tendencies" towards "cosmetics" over content in the cinema today. They remarked, "Today a technological storm is raging, the result of which will be the ultimate democratisation of the cinema." We agree, and now the online film website plugincinema.com is launching the pluginmanifesto, where filmmakers are asked to take advantage of the digital technology revolution.
>
> May 2001, pluginmanifesto launch statement.

The pluginmanifesto arose out of a need. Every time plugincinema was involved in a discussion, conference or talk, the same themes came up. In discussion with others we realized that most people assumed that we were approaching this new technology from the same angle that many others were – that of trying to deliver film or television over the internet. This was not what we were trying to do. We felt that the internet was not just a new viewing platform but a new medium, as different as TV is from film and film is from theatre. The Dogme 95 manifesto offered a challenge to mainstream conventions but did not tackle issues around new technology and the implications for new channels of distribution.[1] This, we reasoned, would require a whole new manifesto.

The Dogme 95 manifesto was about returning to the bare bones of what it saw as filmmaking: storytelling. This involved stripping away the frivolities and apparatus that has become Hollywood. As Thomas Vinterberg, one of the originators of the manifesto, said: 'The emotional life is very explosive, I think this because you have nothing else to tell the story than the actors...you don't have the music to make the crescendo. You have to make them faint, puke or fight."[2] With their vow of chastity, they encouraged filmmakers to abstain from extraneous technology such as additional lighting and special effects. The Dogme manifesto encourages the film-maker to reassess their relationship with technology. To flourish as a filmmaker on the internet necessitates a similar re-evaluation.

To illustrate the idea that different mediums have an effect upon the form that is produced, we will examine the difference between two particular forms: television and film. We can see that they have certain similarities: narrative, a script, direction, lighting, characters and so on. As the younger form, television initially copied film and theatre. Early television borrowed from newsreels, plays were filmed with the camera locked and static to mimic the audience's point of view.

The 1960s play for the BBC, *Cathy Come Home* was the embodiment of television searching for it's own voice and form.[3] It was a combination of documentary and drama, each of which had started in the cinema. However, it was the combination of both that was new. With the advent of docu-drama, television was becoming a medium of gritty realism. Film, with its traditions of large budgets, glamorous stars and lavish sets, evoked far more of a fantasy world than a real one. Television of the 1960s, by contrast, with its real life locations, unknown actors and immediacy, fooled viewers of *Cathy Come Home* into believing it was a documentary and not a drama, thus catapulting social issues into the framework of a realistic drama.

Television has evolved as a medium in its own right; its language can be grasped by the populations who view it across geographical as well as societal divides. There are new forms or programs specific to television: soap operas, situation comedies, game shows, reality TV etc. Because of the addition of audience participation through voting systems, cameras in every room and daily serialisation, phenomena like *Big*

Brother could not exist in a cinematic form.[4] In the end it was video and live broadcast that defined the essential difference between television and the cinema: immediacy.

Reality TV and the internet share certain similar properties, such as multiple web cams, user interaction and immediacy, but the internet has the potential to go even further. As television explores the relatively new medium of the internet, it causes us to reflect upon its evolution. In the way that docu-dramas such as *Cathy Come Home* were part of the defining moments of television in the 1960s, so emerging methods of internet productions are pivotal in evolving the online form.

One such method is Flash, a low bandwidth, easy to use software tool used to create online content.[5] Flash allows a unique mix of both interactive and cinematic tools within the same software package. This dynamic combination highlights the evolutionary potential of such software.

***Elves are for Life*, plugincinema.com, 2001 (Flash)**

The internet is by nature an open, two-way network, and if we can understand this underlying ethos we can understand the way it works. With its roots in military networking, it allows for interconnectivity and access to information in such a way that has been previously impossible. The internet forms a non-hierarchical communication platform, without the usual fixed distribution channels of previous media. Cinema is, in the main, a distribution medium for a small group of very powerful companies. This enables them to broadcast tightly controlled media to a wide audience at a set point and time. TV is similar, though it can have a more localised aspect to it with lip service paid to the involvement of the audience, it is still a distribution medium that distributes from a few to the many. The internet, on the other hand, evolved as a communication medium in which the distribution is a two-way situation as opposed to the 'one-way' broadcasting of TV or passive consumerism of cinema. Consider how news programs function. It is as easy to access current affairs on BBC.co.uk or CNN.com as it is to access an alternative news source such as Indymedia.org or Slashdot.org[6]. However, unlike the BBC or CNN sites, where there is no control over whether your opinion appears on either, both Indymedia and Slashdot are open to all submissions[7]. (In some situations, where message boards and discussion panels feature on a site like the women's forum ivillage.com, for example, the content that the audience contributes may be as important as the input from the creators of the site.)

The pluginmanifesto aims at creating a definitive framework that filmmakers can use to produce films specifically for the internet: to enable them to work with the medium and to see technological limitations as a creative catalyst. While traditional film was hijacked very early on in its career[8], filmmaking for the internet is at a truly inspiring time. Currently, very little exists that has been designed specifically for viewing in this way.

The text of the pluginmanifesto can be freely copied and modified. Indeed we encourage you, along with other filmmakers, artists, self-confessed geeks and web-users, to take the contents of this document and evolve it in-line with your own experiences, ideas and perspectives. This document can be found on the pluginmanifesto homepage at www.pluginmanifesto.com. The document is subject to the Design Science License (DSL) agreement in terms of copying and modifying. Information can be found at http://dsl.org/copyleft/dsl.txt. Please send your modified manifestos to us at plugincinema (info@pluginmanifesto .com) so that we can add your contribution to the pluginmanifesto homepage.

It's time to reclaim film!

Here then it the manifesto that we propose:

The pluginmanifesto version 1.1

It is currently far easier to describe what an online film is not than what it is...

Films are familiar to us all, Hollywood films at least. So much so that it is difficult for us to think about film in any other terms. So we must start with experimentation; play with the conventions. Allow yourself the freedom to move in and out of them, adapting them, using them where appropriate. Freed from prescription, it is easier to see the other possibilities open to us in terms of form and structure as well as content.

A film made for viewing on the internet is not 1_ hours long.

The traditional length of a film – approximately 1 hour 30 minutes – seems right somehow. Much longer and we become restless, much shorter and we feel cheated. Plays also last the same approximate length of time. However, it is the viewing *context* that seems to be the most important element. The short film (10 to 15 minutes) seems an ideal length for the internet. It is the length of time we want to stop for a coffee at work, the length of time we spend having a smoke, or the length of time we don't mind spending viewing a film we don't find easily accessible.

It does not have to have a narrative – structure can come from a variety of means.

Narrative evolved as an intrinsic part of Hollywood filmmaking. Examine other filmmakers such as Deren, Vertov, Godard and Brakhage[9] to see how they structured their films outside the Hollywood narrative tradition. Structure can be created in many ways using colour, music, chapter headings etc. as a shape from which you can hang the images. Or the structure can simply emerge from within the film, by allowing the content to shape itself.

Forget Hollywood...film can be art!

It was decided very early on in the development of the Hollywood ethos that films were products and not art. Independent filmmakers and artists have always known this to be ill-conceived and have preferred to make films with genuine artistic merit. This usually takes place outside of the traditional studio system, although on occasion it happens from within. Film was hijacked very early on in its career. Claim it back! The difference is in the overt aim of the film: whether it is intended to communicate and inform as well as entertain or to simply make money.

Limitations can be creative – if you do not have a wind machine, use a fan. If you do not have the bandwidth, do not expect the cinema.

Filmmaking on the internet is at a truly exciting time. As so little exists that has been designed specifically for viewing on the net, much has been carried across from other mediums such as TV and film. This is not good. It means that the work being shown cannot be appreciated in the form it was originally intended and it also does web films a disservice because audiences complain about the lack of 'quality': their expectations are for the traditional film, seen in its familiar context. In the same way that film found its own form in relation to the theatre, and TV in relation to film, the web filmmaker needs to search for the appropriate form for films on the internet. It is incumbent upon the independent filmmaker to be at the forefront of these new technologies less they be subsumed by the media conglomerates. Independent filmmakers, geeks and artists have an ideal opportunity to experiment and push these technologies creatively and the time is right to do so.

Use codecs and compression creatively.

Use the tools that are appropriate for the job. Filmmaking for the internet is not filmmaking for the cinema. We should be taking the tools invented for the medium such as Flash, html, compression algorithms etc. and pushing them to see what they can do in creative terms: our creative terms. That is the job of the filmmaker and artist. The camera and celluloid defined films for the cinema; computers and the internet will define media for the new millennium.

Filmmakers and geeks should be friends.

Filmmakers, in order to be good at their craft, have always had to have a certain level of technical

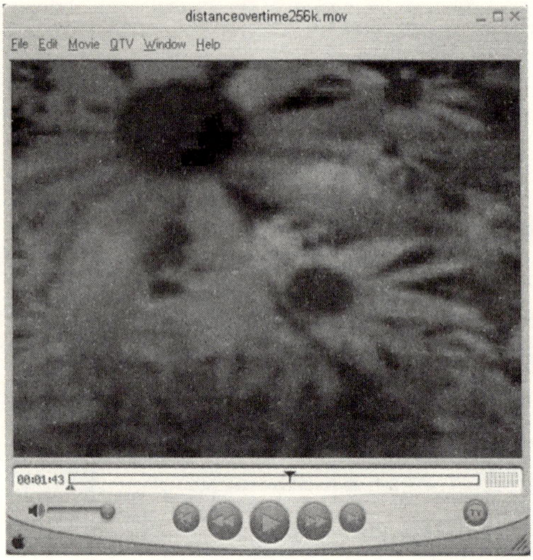

***Distance Over Time*, Dir. Ana Kronschnabl, 2003 (Quicktime)**

knowledge. Many of the short films appearing on the internet have been made by those familiar with the technology, rather than traditional filmmakers. This is no bad thing, however, how much better would those films be if people who had spent their lives learning the craft got together with people who could make the technology work for them? Co-operative and artistic endeavours, the clash of long-term assumptions and traditional approaches with new ideas can produce surprising and challenging new work.

Never forget the medium and the viewing context.

Above all, don't believe the hype! Convergence is certainly happening but the potential of these mediums is only just being glimpsed. What is made for the internet currently can enlighten the forms of the future. The challenge is to create these forms now. This is not a televisual system that sits in the corner of our living rooms, but the internet: a huge system of information storage and retrieval for individual users, with no centralised control. 'Seize the day!' and make your work available to millions of people. Be part of shaping the world's next great art form.

Links for Further Thinking

Design Science License (DSL) by Michael Stutz
http://dsl.org/copyleft/dsl.txt

DOGME 95 Manifesto
http://www.dogme95.bk

pluginmanifesto homepage
http://www.pluginmanifesto.com

plugincinema's five minute guide to Flash technology
http://www.plugincinema.com/plugin/articles/flash.htm

plugincinema's forums to discuss your ideas and practices
http://www.plugincinema.com/plugin/forum

References and Notes

1 The original Dogme 95 manifesto can be found here at **http://www.dogma95.dk**

2 *Dogme 95*, a documentary by Independent Film Channel and Channel 4.

3 BBC1, 1966, directed by Ken Loach. See **http://www.museum.tv/archives/etv/C/htmlC/cathycomeho/cathycomeho.htm** Filmscript for *Cathy Come Home* by Jeremy Sandford available from Marion Boyars Publishers 0-7145-2516-2.

4 *Big Brother* is supposed to be live, but in fact there's a fifteen minute delay which allows programmers to edit it. For more info on *Big Brother* see **http://www.channel4.com/entertainment/tv/microsites/B/bigbrother**

5 Flash is produced by software company Macromedia. **http://www.macromedia.com/software/flash**

6 Indymedia is a worldwide news system that allows the audience to add news without any editorial control. See **http://www.indymedia.org** while Slashdot is a technology news site where the news is gathered though not moderated, by the audience. See **http://slashdot.org**

7 Both sites allow the audience to comment on articles without having to pass through any editorial filter. However, posted comments can be subject to a set degree of editorial input for abusive, sexist and racist content.

8 To research the hijacking of film, read any good book on the history of early cinema.

9 For a starting point you could see the following films: Godard's *Two or Three Things I know about Her* (1968), Vertov's *Man With a Movie Camera* (1929), Deren's *Meshes of the Afternoon* (1943) and Brakhage's *Mothlight* (1963).

DOING

An Introduction to Doing by Robert Newman

Famously in 1977, punk rock fanzine *Sniffin' Glue* once ran a diagram page which listed a series of instructions: cut along dotted line, fold A to B, open flap A to dotted line... NOW FORM A BAND!

It was that simple! Independent punk and new wave bands soon learnt to do it themselves, whereas before we'd been taught to be cowed by the multi-million pound production costs.

As with punk bands, so with the pioneering internet filmmakers now. Suddenly a breach in the hedge has been made, and a way of getting through to a new audience without engaging with the corporate mainstream has been found. A breach where some have been able to make a living out of internet film... And if the living ain't spectacular then so much the better for the work! (After the first $10 million it's hard to make films with passion, one finds. Most damnably hard.) Here is a way for filmmakers to make and control their own work.

And more than that...in fact we enter a wholly new grammar. Maybe 'film' isn't even the word. It's certainly work that's not about trying to ape present formats and tired formulas, only with different, less centralized technology. No, it's summat else entirely. (No matter how much compression you got.) And this is where the exciting artistic and creative challenges spawn and fizz, warped and played and turned and woven symbiotically by a 'weft' and 'woof', uniting concepts like 'copyleft', 'shareware' and 'freeware' with new technologies and a new language of 'film'.

Now that the Information Superhighway does – against all my predictions I admit – appear to be catching on, suddenly the self-mystifying film industry is no longer central.

Robert Newman is an activist, broadcaster, comedian and author of *The Fountain and the Centre of the World* (UK: Verso 2003, US: Soft Skull, 2004). His homepage can be found at http://www.robertnewmancorp.fsnet.co.uk.

Chapter 6: From Idea to Online

A Production Path for Web Films

This chapter describes the entire process involved in the production of a web film, charting each stage from the initial idea through to its distribution on the internet. We have tried to be comprehensive and while a number of the following processes may look daunting, not all of them will be relevant to you. Much will depend upon the type of film you are making and the software you intended to use.

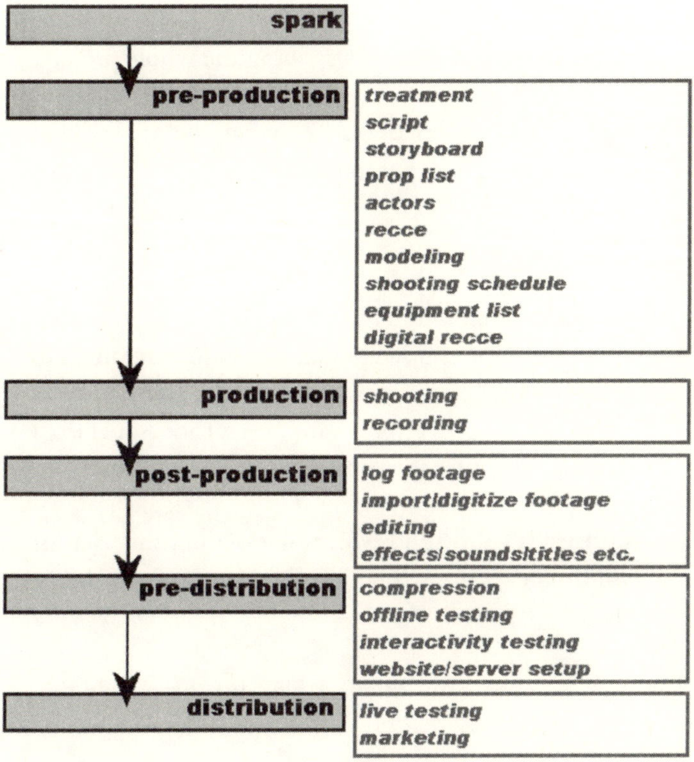

'The Spark'

This is the term used to describe your basic idea and should be a guiding vision for what you hope to achieve, so try and return to it continually throughout the production process in order not to lose sight of your original inspiration.

Pre-Production

This is the planning phase, which is essential. If well executed, it will make filming far quicker and less stressful. Since a web film necessitates additional layers of production, it is even more important to plan things comprehensively (see Chapter 7 for more information). So, here's what your planning phase should include:

Treatment A page or two describing the whole project.

Script A written description of what the viewer will hear, see and do. (For an example of a script see Appendix I.)

Storyboard This uses the script to create a comic strip-like reproduction of the film, with sketched details that describe how the shot will look. It should contain all of the information necessary to make the film, such as shot length, shot description and so on (See Appendix I for an example of a storyboard.)

Prop List If your film involves live action, this is a list of all the items needed within the film, such as chairs, tables, daggers etc.

Actors As above, but this is a plan for the people that are needed.

Recce The process of looking for suitable locations for your film.

Modeling If your film is virtual (i.e. made entirely on a computer), this is a list of all the virtual items and actors needed to make it happen.

Shooting Schedule Shooting is not normally done in narrative order, but in order of location. This is a list of all the scenes arranged by location and time so that you can shoot them efficiently.

Equipment List This differs from the prop list in that it lists all of the technical equipment needed to make the film happen, typically including items such as a DV camera, spare batteries, tripod, gaffer tape, headphones etc.

Digital Recce Make sure you are familiar with all the editing and post-production processes necessary for converting the shot footage into a digital state and have the required skills. It is suggested that you look through Appendices II – V to familiarize yourself with the route. If you are unsure of how to proceed we recommend that you stick to the path laid out by Appendices II, II and V. This gives you a pre-determined path to follow from DV camera to the production of a QuickTime movie.

Production

This is the section where you shoot the film, create the scene or code the interaction (depending on the nature of your film).

Shooting The name given to the process of using a camera to acquire the footage needed for the film.

Recording This is where any music or voiceovers are recorded.

Post-Production

Here, the filmmaker takes what is created in the production stage, 'the rushes' (the name given to the raw footage taken during the shoot) and attempts to turn this material into a coherent and finished product ie: the film.

Log Footage A process where the rushes are viewed and a record made of every shot. This log is vital when selecting which shots to use during the editing process and for checking that all the scenes needed to tell the story have been shot. You need to document (for each tape) the time the shot begins and ends, and include a brief description of the contents of each shot.

Import/Digitize Footage Once you have logged all the footage (this is obviously only applicable if you are working with a camera), you will need to import or capture the relevant shots into your computer.(For an example of capturing see Appendix II). By using the log you made, you can ensure that you only import the footage you need. Remember, once imported, the hard-disk requirements of uncompressed footage can be considerable. (See Chapter 12 for more information).

Editing Editing is the process of converting the storyboard into the final film. Here the footage is cut up; with transitions and certain effects added. Modern editing software such as Premiere, Blade Final Cut Pro or VirtualDub allows the process to be conducted non-linearly as opposed to traditional linear methods.[1](See Chapter 7 for more information and for a guide to editing see Appendix III.)

Effects, Sounds, Titles etc Effects such as layering or filters can be applied to the footage using software such as Final Cut Pro or After Effects.[2] These are more advanced effects that manipulate the digital footage to create features of added interest. Layering is the placing of one or more layers of footage on top of another, to be played at the same time, with a varying degree of transparency, to create interesting effects. Filters are processes that are applied to footage, again to enhance the image quality in some way: the filter may change the colour or the contrast and add any number of interesting effects.

Sound can also be added during the editing process by importing the digitized file into the software and placing it on the time-line in the same way as image files. Titles can be created using an art package such as Photoshop or Paint Shop Pro and the results imported into the appropriate editing software.[3] (There are restrictions on file types depending on the software being used so remember to check for this when you do your digital recce.) (See Appendix III for an example of an image being imported into editing software to act as a title.)

Pre-distribution

This is where the film is prepared for distribution on the internet.

Compression This is where the film is built (or exported) using the editing software and made more appropriate for distribution on the internet (see Chapter 10).

Offline Testing Once the compressed film has been produced, the filmmaker should try to view it using various different media players. This will give an idea of the compatibility of your film and what instructions (if any) you might need to give on a website to enable people to view it easily. (For more information on the various media players available see Chapter 2.)

Interactivity Testing If the film has an interactive component then this needs to be tested to ensure that all the elements function correctly.

Website/Server Setup You will need to set up the web infrastructure required to distribute your film, which could involve a server, website or peer-to-peer system. (See Appendix IV.)

Distribution

These are the processes that need to be considered once your film has gone 'live'.

Live Testing Once your films, and any associated files, have been uploaded to the internet, you will need to check that your efforts have been successful. Try accessing the film from a friend's computer, remembering that if you are intending to make the work accessible over a 56K modem, it obviously needs to be tested by attempting to view it over a 56K connection.[4] The experience will differ considerably if the film is intended for viewing over Broadband as opposed to a 56K modem.

Marketing Once you have tested everything online, it can be considered 'live' and accessible to the public. The task of promoting your film is a huge topic in its own right, however, a good starting place would be to look at the successes of previous projects that have exploited the strengths of the internet, such as *The Blair Witch Project* or Steven Spielberg's *AI.*[5]

The Blair Witch Project famously used the internet to generate its own hype. Enthusiastic tales of the film's spine-chilling terror and gushing praise for its realistic camerawork were generated, allegedly by the makers, to sell the project both to a film distributor and to the public at large. *AI* on the other hand, had a marketing campaign that centred around the film's content. Through the use of fake websites and newsgroup postings, they created an online narrative. It was designed to involve the audience to such an extent that seeing the film became the final leg of a journey they had begun online.

Links for Further Doing

plugincinema's 'Frequently Asked Questions'
http://www.plugincinema.com/plugin/film_school/pluginfaq.htm

plugincinema's 'Glossary of Terms'
http://www.plugincinema.com/plugin/glossary

plugincinema's 'Interactive Story Board Exercise'
http://www.plugincinema.com/plugin/film_school/interactive.html

RobWalker.net 'The Blair Witch Myth'
http://robwalker.net/html_docs/blair.html

Salon.com 'Did The Blair Witch Project fake its online fan base?'
http://www.salon.com/tech/feature/1999/07/16/blair_marketing

Wired.com 'A.I.: Unravelling the Mysteries'
http://www.wired.com/news/digiwood/0,1412,44868,00.html

References and Notes

1 Final Cut Pro is produced by Apple and more information on it can be found at **http://www.apple.com/finalcutpro.** Premiere is produced by Adobe and more information can be found here **http://www.adobe.com/products/premiere/main.html** while Blade is

produced by In-Sync and more info can be found here http://www.in-sync.com

2 Final Cut Pro is produced by Apple and more information on it can be found here http://www.apple.com/finalcutpro After Effects is produced by Adobe and more information and be found at http://www.adobe.com/products/aftereffects/main.html

3 Photoshop is produced by Adobe and more information on it can be found here http://www.adobe.com/products/photoshop/main.html Paint Shop Pro is produced by Jasc Software and more information on it can be found here http://www.jasc.com

4 For more information on the various types of internet connection see the plugincinema article, 'Connecting to the internet 101.' http://www.plugincinema.com/plugin/film_school/guide_to_internet.htm

5 There are lots of interesting articles on *The Blair Witch Project*. Some that are worth taking a look at include: '*The Blair Witch Project.'* from *Film Quarterly*, Spring 2001 by J.P. Telotte at http://www.findarticles.com/cf_0/m1070/3_54/74800528/p2/article.jhtml?term=%22blair+witch%22 and 'The *Blair Witch* Myth' RbWalker.net at http://robwalker.net/html_docs/blair.html or 'Did The *Blair Witch* Myth fake its online fan base?' by Patrizia DiLucchio http://www.salon.com/tech/feature/1999/07/16/blair_marketing For Spielberg's *A.I.* see the *Wired* article '*A.I*: Unravelling the Mysteries,' at http://www.wired.com/news/digiwood/0,1412,44868,00.html

Chapter 7: The Production Process

Introduction

Production is the process of ensuring that everything in the project that is supposed to happen, happens on time, and that all the required components of the film work together as planned. A successful production process ensures that the original idea is followed through to completion while enabling the creative vision to shine.

Production on web films requires something of a paradigm shift. In the traditional model, exemplified by Hollywood, budgets are huge and production becomes the responsibility of a sizeable team rather than one or two individuals. For our purposes, production is more akin to that found in independent/low budget filmmaking. The small scale of the operation means that those involved will often adopt several roles and thus be required to multi-skill. Orson Welles is an infamous (and talented) exemplar of the multi-skilled filmmaker,[1] as he was involved with writing, producing and directing as well as acting. (He was also involved in the business side of film production, as a co-founder of the Society of Independent Motion Picture Producers.[2])

Production is vital whether the project involves an individual working away at a computer or a team of twenty people collaborating on a project. This point cannot be overstated: without production there is no organisation to the project and without organisation the project's viability is in question. Planning and organisation can make the difference between bringing an idea to completion and the abandonment of the project altogether. While there will always be unforeseen difficulties and technical hitches, this chapter aims to ensure that the negative impact of these factors is minimised, enabling the creative vision behind the project to achieve its full potential.

The most comprehensive approach towards production

for a web film is to break it down into its constituent parts. These can be categorised by the following three headings: *pre-production*, *production* and *post-production*. A full breakdown of the process can be found in Chapter 6, however, in this chapter we will take a closer look at some of the most important production issues.

Pre-Production

The Spark Unsurprisingly, considering it name, this starts with a spark of an idea and immediately requires that you begin thinking about the medium; indeed, thinking about the medium itself might be the germination of the idea. For example, the way the compression algorithms affected fur inspired the use of this effect as the basis of the film *George the Mewvie.*[3]

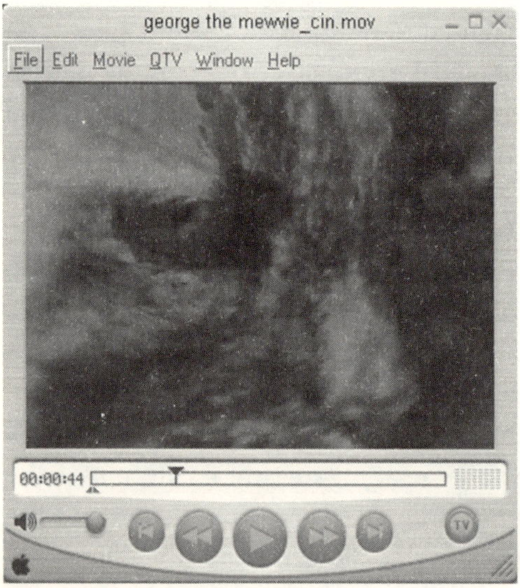

George the Mewvie, Dir. Ana Kronschnabl, 2002 (QuickTime)

In web filmmaking, to achieve a successful integration of the technological, aesthetic and practical components in question, the production process must be carefully considered from the very start. For example, if you were thinking of doing an interactive film, you should consider using Flash[4]. The format you choose will have a variety of implications for the production process, raising questions such as: 'Would this story be best told in animation or though video footage?' If you wish to create a grainy 1920s feel you might wish to shoot the footage on an old-fashioned camera such as Super8 but you would then need to consider how this would be digitized. Shooting on DV (digital video) then using a filter in the editing process to re-create the aesthetic you desire may be an easier way of achieving the result you want, but possibly not as much fun.

Treatment Once you have the idea and are thinking about the medium, you need to write what is known as a 'treatment'. A treatment is a description of what the project is, i.e.: the idea, length, medium and estimated size of the finished file, all of which affect the way you are able to distribute the file. A treatment is usually only necessary when pitching the idea or applying for funding from some professional body or another, but will neatly sum up all the various aspects of your work which you should be keeping in mind. Although there are many different approaches to writing a treatment, in this chapter the method is modified to fit with the web filmmaking aesthetic.

Script As you will already be aware, a script is the written version of your work, be it drama/animation/film/performance or otherwise. Unlike a standard story or a novel, a script is a transitional piece of work and is destined (we hope) to become a web film. Although most of the available literature intended to guide you through scriptwriting relates to writing for film or TV, it's worth glancing at, as attempting to write a script, even for a short film, can be a daunting task. The most important thing to remember is that there are no hard and fast rules: become familiar with existing scriptwriting conventions so that you will be able to use them where appropriate but do not be afraid to discard them when necessary. (See Appendix I.)

Production

In the following section, we've listed a few useful tricks of the trade, gleaned from experienced filmmakers and producers to help your filmmaking run more smoothly. Some may seem self-explanatory and barely in need of attention, but have been included since it is all too easy to overlook the glaringly obvious:

Murphy's Law of Filmmaking Everything will always take twice as long as you expect; especially when planning your shooting schedule. Draw up a timetable that leaves plenty of leeway, as you will most likely find that technical hitches and other random problems and errors will constantly drain the allotted time away.

Backups Equipment critical to the shooting process has a tendency to go wrong when you most need it. Determine which items are most important to your project, such as scripts, cameras, batteries and sound equipment, and make sure they are absolutely ready to go (charged, tested and so on). Where possible make sure that you also have back-ups to enable the production to continue should the worst happen.

Food and Drink You will be able to keep people working hard and their morale high if you can keep a good supply of hot, tasty food and suitable drinks on site. This is especially true of small budget productions where you may not be able to pay people the going rate for their efforts.[5]

Reducing Uncertainties Take time to look through the documents you have created and think through the whole process in your mind. Look for holes in what you are doing and try to fill them. Do not leave it until the last minute to fix things; be pro-active about it. Prevention is better than cure!

Feedback Your team will need firm direction to ensure consistency is maintained but keep loads of positive feedback coming. People always respond well to praise and encouragement where due and it will keep morale high. As a simple rule of thumb, if you see or know of somebody who has done a good job, take the time to say so.

Good Communication If people find they are unaware of what is happening, they will loose faith in the project and it will hinder the production process. If a decision is to be made that affects other people, make sure everybody knows about it as soon as possible. This will help keep the whole filmmaking process open and transparent enabling problems to come to the surface as soon as they appear.

Inconsistency If you make a decision, stick to it. Nothing hinders progress more than indecisive and inconsistent behaviour. Weigh decisions carefully before you make them but do not be afraid to make important decisions.

Summary

Recent studies by the psychologist G.L.Caxton show how

creativity flourishes when individuals feel free from pressure and stress.[6] Good production is a vital area; hundreds of pages of beautifully scripted dialogue and a top of the range camera and equipment will not save a film if the production process fails. Conversely, if the production is good and the atmosphere created is a positive, well-oiled machine, then creativity will flourish.

Links for Further Doing

plugincinema.com's 'Guide to Production'
http://www.plugincinema.com/plugin/film_school/production_1.htm

plugincinema.com's 'Guide to Script Writing'
http://www.plugincinema.com/plugin/film_school/script_1.htm

Scr(i)pt Magazine
http://www.scriptmag.com

Script Layout
http://www.dramaplus.org/script.htm

References and Notes

1 For more information see the site of the estate of Orson Welles
http://www.bway.net/~nipper/home.html

2 For the April 13, 1942 statement by the Society of Independent Motion Picture Producers see the link to Cobbles.com at
http://www.cobbles.com/simpp_archive/simpp_1942pressrelease.htm

3 It wasn't that I made it with any particular player in mind, however, from previous experience I knew the 'approximate' affect compression would have on the film as a whole. I also used a variety of different codecs and compressed it in a whole range of ways to experiment and find the one I liked the look of the best. *George the Mewvie* can be seen at
http://www.plugincinema.com/plugin/plugin_cinema/index.htm#f26

4 Flash is produced by Macromedia http://www.macromedia.com

5 Remember that you may have alternative dietary requirements such as vegetarians on your team: cater for them!

6 For more on this see the plugincinema article http://www.plugincinema.com/plugin/film_school/production_1.htm

Chapter 8: Tools of the Trade

What to Look For

In this chapter we discuss the tools that are appropriate when making a film for the internet. Perhaps you need a whole studio, chairs with 'director' stencilled on them or a crew so large you need to employ caterers and security? Maybe you just use a PC? There are a variety of options and its up to you to choose the equipment that best suits your project (and budget). As all your work will eventually be imported into the digital domain, one factor you will need to consider is the chain of events that get you there – remembering that creation can take place in either the real world or the digital world.

> **The Real World** Here you need some type of capture device such as a camera but anything from Super8 to a DV (Digital Video) camera will do. You may be using actors, filming a cat or using Claymation, the important point is that you have a clear idea of what you want and intend to use some form of technology to capture it. (See Appendix II for an example of capturing.)

> **The Digital World** Here you are either creating your ideas from scratch using art and animation software or building your ideas inside a PC using software such as Flash, 3DStudio Max or Director.[1] You may wish to sample work from existing film or files of photography, in which case your content is already within the digital realm. The only thing you need to do is to check that the format is compatible with the software you are using.

You could use a mixture of different forms, for example mixing footage from a Pixelvision camera with DV and 3D animation.[2] (Pixelvision is the name for the PXL-200 video camera that was made by Fisher-Price in the 1980s and which produces a very particular type of low-quality images. It uses ordinary cassette tapes to record audio and video and fits about 5 minutes for footage onto each side of the tape.) Of course, this approach may require further work in order to make the content compatible, and you will also need to consider whether the technology you have chosen to use is digital or analogue, but the results can be worth the extra effort.

Digital vs. Analogue

Some cameras you may use will shoot in DV while others may be older analogue technologies such as Super8 or VHS. For a precise definition of the difference between digital and analogue see 'Links for Further Doing' at the end of this chapter. For our current purposes, however, the difference becomes particularly relevant in the editing and copying stages as follows. Analogue footage is pieced together along a timeline in order. The footage (source) is physically copied from one tape to another (master). If you are halfway through the film and wish to change the beginning, you generally have to start again.

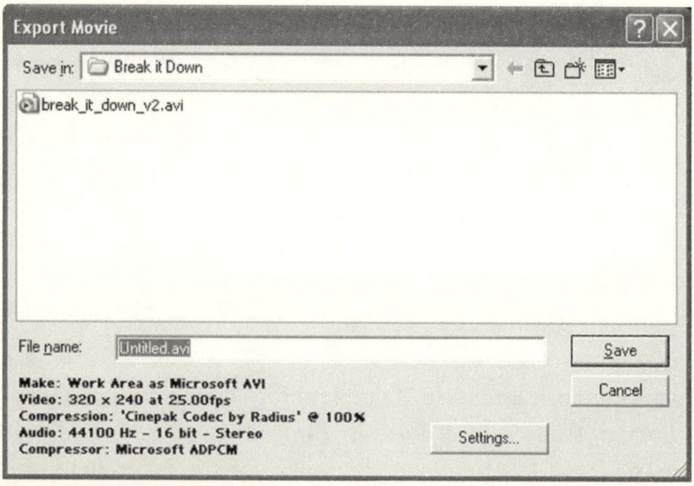

The export screen in Premiere 6

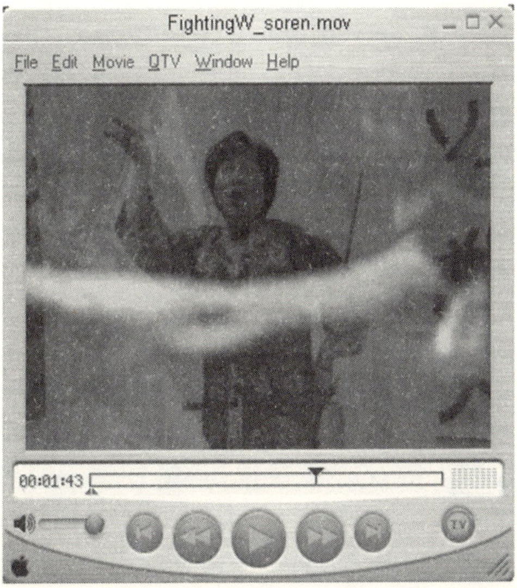

***Fighting Women II*, Dir. Ana Kronschnabl, 2001 (QuickTime)**

On the other hand, when editing digitally there are no changes to the original footage. The software remembers the editing information as separate data and it is only when you make the final movie that the information is manipulated and the film is created.

As the copying of digital information is supposedly 'lossless,' (i.e. loses nothing from the original) there should be no reduction in picture quality when editing digitally.[3] Analogue editing, by nature, involves one generation of image degradation.

There is much debate concerning the quality of analogue verses digital as a recording medium. There are differences, but each format has its own look and feel. You must choose the one that is most appropriate for your needs, both practically and artistically. (See plugincinema's *Fighting Women II* as an example of mixing analogue and digital footage.)[4] It's really a very personal thing. As filmmakers we like to use whichever medium seems to lend itself to the project. For example, in *Fighting Women II* a variety of different acquisition mediums have been used, ranging from Super8 through to footage captured from a computer game, recorded onto VHS and then digitized. This is a personal choice, however, and is more of a reflection upon a particular, rather eclectic, way of working. It could be argued that this aesthetic is far less purist than that of traditional experimental filmmaking where celluloid is the essential element.

If you are filming with DV, the process is much more straightforward. Not only are DV cameras easy to use and lightweight but as they capture images digitally, there will be one less step in the process of transferring images to a computer to worry about. The footage can be exported directly into the machine via a digital linking cable (such as FireWire aka IEEE 1394)[5] or an analogue cable.

Flash

We will now look at how the creation of ideas takes place within the computer. One of the most widely used packages for creating web films is Macromedia's software, 'Flash'. Flash is an all-in-one animation and editing package that creates interactive animations that are small both in terms of memory and download size. The ability to watch Flash animations is currently installed on 3000+ million computers worldwide, and all major web-browsers now have the necessary Flash player built-in as standard. Part of Flash's popularity comes from the fact that it is relatively simple to use; creating animated films can be a quick process and once you have produced the basic components of your work, creating additional material using these components becomes even easier. For example, in the plugincinema film *Elves are for Life* each elf shares the same body with the others. This means only one body, one hand and one head needs to be made for the whole workshop full of elves – each elf being created from re-sized, re-coloured and re-positioned duplicates.

***Elves are for Life*, plugincinema.com, 2001 (Flash)**

The resultant film will also be in a form that has been optimised for showing on the internet. Even if you do not wish to work with animation ultimately, it makes a great tool for creating storyboards and for prototyping ideas. Flash enables you to bring your vision to life without committing expensive resources to it, and seeing if your idea works out on screen before filming even begins.

Editing

Once you have produced the content and gathered it all together, the next stage is editing; generally known as post-production, this is the stage at which you follow your plan or storyboard. If the footage has been gathered using analogue film equipment you may choose to edit in the same format, alternatively, you can import the raw footage into a computer and edit the piece digitally. Editing on a personal computer, with software such as Final Cut Pro or Premiere, provides an ability to manipulate the overall look of the film in a way that would be impossible with analogue post-production methods.

As you can see, it is preferable to use a non-linear system for editing web films (mainly because of the final output needing to be in a digital form for distribution), and the further advantage of such a method is that it can be done using your own PC. You will need to select the software you are going to use to edit with and this decision is complex as there are a huge number of competing editing packages vying for your attention. These include Adobe's Premiere, In-Snyc's Blade and Apple's Final Cut Pro.[6] (Ultimately, the programme you opt for is a personal choice, akin to preferring a mac to a PC for example.) There are also a number of free software tools such as Virtual Dub, which runs on windows as well as other software platforms, and the Linux video editing tool Cinelerra.[7]

It is difficult to recommend specific editing software as it depends on both the computer and the operating system you are running, and how demanding your editing needs are. However, there are certain points you should be aware of. Firstly, when selecting an editing system, ensure that you check the requirements of the software vs. your own system. These requirements typically list the type of processor, amount of RAM memory and hardrive space you require to run it. If you don't meet the standard that the software manufacture recommends, then don't go there! There is nothing more frustrating that fighting your computer's limitations when trying to edit – it is a hard enough job as it is!

Secondly, try out evaluation versions of the software where possible first. You can often download demo or limited versions of programs from a manufacturer's website, or from the cover discs of computer magazines. Open Source or free software obviously has a particular advantage in terms of price. Once you have obtained the software try out the different packages and see how easy it is to use each one; is it intuitive for the way you like to work? Also, look into the help files provided by each package; this can make all the difference between being able to use the software at a complex level or never figuring out how to get it to fade to black!

Thirdly, it is worth considering the level of complexity that you require. If you only require the most basic of editing facilities, a possible solution might be one of the very basic packages on the market. An example of this might be to use one of the enhanced versions of a proprietary media player for simple editing tasks; for example QuickTimePro 6.5 has simple editing options such as cut, copy and paste as well as being able to import and export video from around a dozen file formats, including the DV and MPEG-4. Apple distribute this as an online upgrade to their QuickTime player for a small fee.

Finally, and most importantly, make sure that the software you are selecting has the ability to both import your footage and export the final movie in the format you require.

Choosing Your Tools

As we have discussed, there is a myriad of choices when making a web film. How do you set about narrowing down the options? The following points are worth considering:

What You've Got Do not waste time considering options you do not have access to; think in terms of what you know you can get hold of and your ambitions will be much more achievable. This is a similar sentiment to the one expressed by Robert Rodriguez (director of *Desperado, Spy Kids* and *El Mariachi*) in his '10 Minute Film School': 'Look around you, what do you have around you? Take stock of what you have. Your father owns a liquor store – make a movie about a liquor store. Do you have a dog? Make a movie about your dog. Your mom works in a nursing home, make a movie about a nursing home.'[8] All he had was a tortoise and an empty guitar case when he made the cult film *El Mariachi.*

Digitizing It You need to consider the practicalities of getting your work into the digital realm. If you chose to use a Super8 camera, can you get the footage into a computer? One option would be to find a photo processing shop that offers this as a service. Another option would be to project the Super8 footage and film it yourself using a DV camera. The first option may produce a better quality image but would be more expensive, whereas the second would be virtually free provided you have access to the equipment.

Suitability Are the medium and equipment you have chosen suitable for the film you wish to make? The nature of this question is less practical and more of an aesthetic one. Do they have the right look for the style of web film you want to make? For instance, if it is animation, have you considered Animation Shop?[9] This software may be especially appropriate if you are intending to create small banner ad style animations. If not this, Flash might be the tool to look at? If you are making a spoof television advert, have you looked into DV? This point is covered in Chapter 5. Suffice to say the digitising process is an extremely important one, as it will have a notable effect on the overall appearance and sound of the final piece.

Planning the Edit At this stage you have to ask yourself if you are ready for the post-production phase of your web film: do you understand the software and how to link it to the relevant hardware? If your DV camera has FireWire output, does your computer have a matching input? If your DV camera uses a USB 2.0 port, does your computer have this port too? If not, can your computer be upgraded to allow the two to be linked? (For an example of capturing footage from DV see Appendix II.) After the initial plans have been made take some time to realistically reassess the viability of the project, asking, for example: is the time-scale realistic? If there are expenses, how will you raise the money? Do you need to be more realistic and cut back on some of your more expensive ideas? Do you need to come up with a more appropriate timescale? The more honest you are with yourself at this stage, the more likely it will be that your film gets made.

Summary

If anything in this chapter has seemed confusing, do not worry: many of the topics touched on here will be explored in greater detail and including more technical depth in other chapters. What we hope you have taken away from this section is a general idea of how you will translate your vision into raw footage and finally into a finished film (or what research is necessary to obtain one). This list, for example, outlines one simple route that could be followed from footage acquisition though to a web film:

1. Use a DV camera to acquire both footage and sound
2. Capture from the camera into the PC by a connection known as FireWire.
3. Use a software package such as Premiere to edit the film.
4. Export the edited footage into an internet appropriate format such as QuickTime. See Appendix V for an example of encoding using this format.

At this point it is worth mentioning the requirements your computer will need in order to manipulate digital video. It is always worth checking with your computer manufacturer, but the essentials are:

- A fast processor and plenty of RAM (1.70 GHz-M and 512 megabytes of RAM or greater).

- A large hardrive for storage (40 Gigabytes or more, with 72,000 RPM or more). A hardrive is the component of a computer that acts as the permanent storage space.
- Capture Card (PCI capture card. Some laptops have built-in capture capability). A capture card is the name given to a device, often installed inside the computer, that provides an extra port which the complementing device (in this case a DV camera) can plug into. This may be already installed in your computer.
- FireWire or IEEE 1394 (comes as standard with most computers). This would be the type of port suggested. You should be looking for a computer with this port already installed or the capture card (above) to have this port.
- DV editing software (Premiere, Final Cut Pro, VirtualDubMod, Blade etc.).

Links for Further Doing

Plugincinema's equipment & software guides
http://www.plugincinema.com/plugin/equipment/

plugincinema's Flash guide
http://www.plugincinema.com/plugin/articles/flash.htm

plugincinema's 'How to put VHS footage onto the Web'
http://www.plugincinema.com/plugin/film_school/vhs.htm

plugincinema's '5 Minute Guide to Digital vs. Analogue'
http://www.plugincinema.com/plugin/articles/digitalvsanalogue.htm

Robert Rodriguez's '10 Minute Film School'
http://www.exposure.co.uk/makers/minute.html

plugincinema's *Fighting Women II*
http://www.plugincinema.com/plugin/plugin_cinema/index.htm#f15

References and Notes

1 Flash and Director are made by Macromedia, see http://www.macromedia.com and 3D Studio Max is made by Discreet, see http://www.discreet.com Flash has been designed to produce interactivity and animated content for internet. 3DStudio Max is primarily modelling software that is used to produce computer generated 3D models as well as being useful for simulating the environment eg lighting or movement on the model. Director is primarily software that is used to create interactive CD-ROMs and DVDs.

2 A few years after the emergence of Pixelvision in the late 1980s, Pixelvision pieces started showing up at film and video festivals and it has since developed quite a cult following. From http://elvis.rowan.edu/~cassidy/pixel

3 There are a variety of errors that can occur during the transfer of digital data that can corrupt it. For more on 'lossless' transference see Chapter 10.

4 See plugincinema's *Fighting Women II* as an example of mixing

analogue and digital footage on .
http://www.plugincinema.com/plugin/plugin_cinema/index.htm#f15

5 For more on FireWire/IEEE 1394, see
http://www.webopedia.com/TERM/I/IEEE_1394.html and
http://www.apple.com/firewire

6 For information on Premiere see
http://www.adobe.com/products/premiere/main.html and for information on Final Cut Pro see http://www.apple.com/finalcutpro and for information on Blade see http://www.in-sync.com

7 For more on VirtualDub see http://www.virtualdub.org and for more on Cinelerra http://heroinewarrior.com/cinelerra.php3

8 The full text of Robert Rodriguez's '10 Minute Film School' is available here http://www.exposure.co.uk/makers/minute.html

9 Animation Shop id a GIF animation package made by JASC, see http://www.jasc.com

10 The computer's processor determines the speed at which it operates. RAM or Random Access Memory is the amount of data that can be processed in real-time.

Chapter 9: Advice on Cameras

Introduction

Being the most crucial part of a traditional shooting kit, it is worth familiarising yourself with your camera. This shouldn't prove difficult as most cameras are very similar in functionality; even the jump from analogue to digital created few dramatic differences in basic camera design. You will be able to identify simple function buttons like the record and zoom buttons without any trouble. There is often a different set of functions with DV cameras that is accessible via an on screen menu, giving control over the shutter speed for example, although this will vary from camera to camera. It is a good idea to initially read only as much of the manual as you need to understand the basics, then read further as you come across particular problems you need to solve or ideas you wish to experiment with. The following section covers some of the points you may wish to consider, whether you are undecided as to which camera to buy, or wish to become familiar with the one you already own.

Camera Compatibility

There are a couple of questions you need to ask yourself to begin with. Are the camera and PC you intend to buy compatible with each other? Is the connection on the camera (e.g. FireWire, USB 2.0 etc.) the same as your PC?[1] In theory any digital appliance should work with any other, but in practice, different brands can conflict and different devices can come with a variety of connections. Ask friends whom you know have brought similar equipment and see what they chose. If you are making an in-store purchase, ask the sales assistant to demonstrate that the connectivity and functionality they describe really does work.

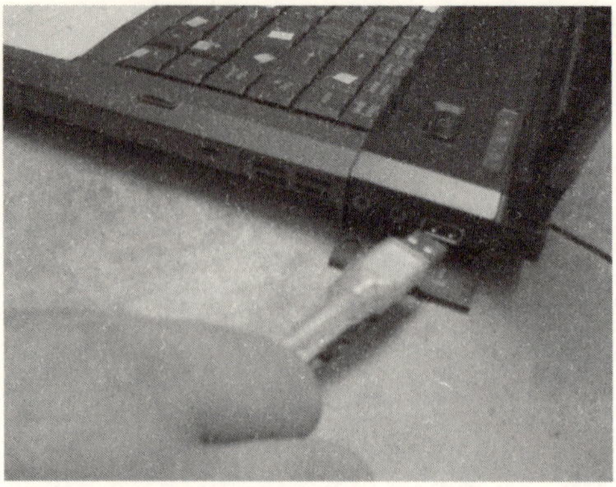

USB connection on a PC laptop.

Get a Tripod

Whilst filming, even small movements of the arm can translate into very jerky looking footage. This is fine if you are aiming for a *Hills Street Blues* look, but you have to remember that the footage you shoot will need to be compressed and this style of fast moving camera work has implications for this process (covered in Chapter 12).[2] Whatever your intentions, it is always a good idea to get the best footage you can, which means using a tripod; though the decision is an aesthetic one and finally comes down to artistic direction.

White Balance

This is a process where you 'tell' the camera what white is; it is done to maintain a standard white throughout the footage despite the differences in the temperature of the light within each shot (temperature in filmmaking refers to the warm/cold look to the light). Following this procedure will ensure that all of your footage has a continuous feel to it. Most DV cameras are set to automatically white balance the footage but you may wish to check to see if your camera has this function, or even experiment with it. You can have fun playing with the white balance, for example you could try convincing the camera that red is actually white creating footage with a far darker feel.

Lighting

If you are choosing a DV camera, you are probably already at an advantage, as they are often designed to operate in low light conditions. Some even have a form of light enhancing 'night vision'. By all means experiment with your camera's performance in natural lighting conditions (i.e. with no additional lighting), but if its not up to producing film of the quality you are looking for, you may want to consider additional spotlights. Just remember, overloading yourself with equipment is a sure way of removing one of the advantages a web filmmaker has. There are definite advantages to a lightweight, portable kit! Note the advice of Dogme 95 filmmakers Lars von Trier and Thomas Vinterberg, 'Special lighting is not acceptable. (If there is too little light for exposure the scene must be cut or a single lamp be attached to the camera).'[3] There is more discussion of this manifesto in Chapter 5.

Sound

It is also a good idea to experiment with various methods of recording sound, as this is an often overlooked but important area. There is no point in agonising over a script or tweaking dialogue to perfection if, when you come to shoot the scene, nobody can hear what is being said. Most modern VHS and DV cameras have at least one built in microphone. Ideally you want to be looking for a camera with two mic inputs, as this allows you to both use the inbuilt mic and take an input from a second external mic: perhaps a lapel, lavalier or clip-on mic (this is a type of microphone designed specifically to record conversation, attached to each speaker to capture conversations without being intrusive) or a PZM or boundary effect microphone (used to pick up ambient sound when placed on reflective surfaces, useful for reducing the amount of echo in a large space).

The above camera has only one sound channel; the external mic overrides the internal camera mic.

And Finally...

In summary, it is essential that you make sure you know how (or if) your chosen camera does the things you need it to do. Do not worry if at first this seems complicated, just experiment and keep experimenting until you are comfortable with your equipment.

Links for Further Doing

Apple's Firewire
http://www.apple.com/firewire

Camcorder User
http://www.camuser.co.uk

plugincinema's equipment & software guides
http://www.plugincinema.com/plugin/equipment

USB 2.0
http://www.usb.org/developers/usb20

References and Notes

1 For more information on FireWire, see http://www.apple.com/firewire and for more information on USB 2.0 see http://www.usb.org/home/faq

2 'Quick cuts, a furious pace, a nervous camera made for complexity and congestion, a sense of entanglement and continuous crisis that matched the actual density and convolution of city life.' http://www.museum.tv/archives/etv/H/htmlH/hillstreetb/hillstreetb.htm

3 From Dogme 95 'Vow of Chastity': Rules 1-10, d. http://faculty.washington.edu/akn/lecture36009.htm

Chapter 10: Compression

Why Do We Need Compression?

Compression is the name given to the various processes that are used to make digital files smaller, and therefore more easily transferable over the internet. When you are dealing with a file (such as a film) that is considerably larger than the medium it is intended for, a number of steps must be taken to ensure that this method of transportation is a realistic option.[1]

Forms of Compression

There are two main forms of compression used on the internet, known as 'lossy compression' and 'lossless compression'. The difference between the two relates to their reversibility: with lossless compression it is possible to return to the original uncompressed form whereas with lossy compression it is not. In this chapter we examine the issues surrounding the latter because this is the form with the most obvious impact on filmmaking for the internet. However, as both share a common approach to data compression, it is helpful to understand some of this methodology. In most cases, compression works by looking for the common elements within the data. These common elements are known as 'redundancy'. Compression is then able to reduce the amount of storage space needed to describe this redundant data. The more redundant data a file contains, the greater the degree of compression that can be applied. The best way to understand these ideas is to see them in action:

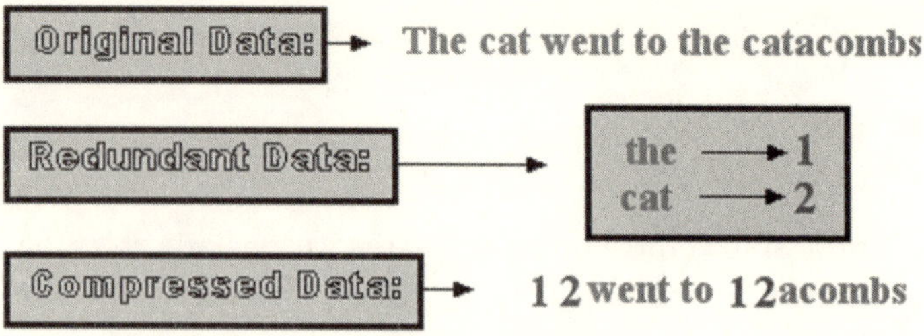

In this example the words 'cat' and 'the' are the redundant data in the sentence. To compress, they are given the codes 1 and 2, respectively, to represent them. This substitution shrinks the original sentence of 24 characters, to one of only 16 characters. This simple example uses a technique known as 'run length encoding', which is one of many different methods used to compress data.[2]

Examining Lossy and Lossless Compression

In the above example, once you know the method used to compress the data, you can easily reconstruct the original sentence. This is known as 'lossless compression' which, as mentioned, involves the data being processed into a compressed form and decompressed back into the original form with no loss of quality. You will find that one of the most frequent encounters with lossless compression occurs when you use a 'zip' compression utility to make data smaller e.g. using software such as Winzip or Ultimate Zip.[3] On the other hand, as lossy compression means that there is a degradation of the original data, once compressed it can never be returned to its original state. This is because lossy compression involves some of the original data being lost forever during the process. This may sound a worse option, however, lossy compression has an important advantage; the compressed form is still intelligible without the file being decompressed (this is especially useful when applied to images).

If you consider the original sentence we compressed earlier: '1 2 went to 1 2acombs' in its compressed form does not make much sense, so it needs to be decompressed before it can be understood.[4] Similarly a zipped file cannot have its contents examined while it is zipped up – it must be unzipped before it can be used.

Compressing Still Images

As previously stated, data that has been subject to lossy compression can be examined while compressed, this has important uses when large data files need to be transferred in an intelligible form. The most common form of lossy compression that people encounter on the internet is through viewing images.

Below are some sample images that have been subject to lossy intraframe compression.[5] This means that the lossy compression has been applied to each image individually. You can see from the images, as more compression is added, that the file size of the image decreases, alongside the quality of the image. (The examples below use JPEG compression, which is discussed later in this chapter.)

Uncompressed image (file size – 198 KB)

JPEG image with 50% compression setting (file size – 13 KB)

JPEG image with 100% compression setting (file size – 4 KB)

You will notice blurred patches appearing in the image where the application of compression technology has resulted in a noticeable loss of quality that jars with the eye. Such effects are known as 'artifacting'.

In addition to applying compression technology, the file size of an image can be lowered by simply shrinking the size of the image.

Another factor that relates to the size and appearance of the image is of course colour. The more colours the image uses, the more data is required to store this information and so the larger the file size.

Uncompressed image with 16 million colour resolution (file size – 198 KB)

GIF image with 64-colour setting (file size – 19 KB)

produce a sizeable file. In the example of the JPEG 100% fully compressed image used above, it would be indicative of a single frame in a one second film at the PAL standard of 25 frames per second and would therefore be a considerably larger file (100 KB).

It is clear that with such file sizes resulting, it is necessary to further compress moving image files to make them even smaller. The processes used to achieve this additional layer of compression are broadly termed interframe compression.[7]

Interframe compression uses a variety of methods: the number of frames per second can be lowered (a technique known as sub-sampling). If the frame rate were reduced to

Uncompressed image with dimensions 300 x 225 pixels (file size – 198 KB) (A pixel is the smallest recognizable element of a digital image, a tiny dot of colou

Uncompressed image with dimensions 180 x 135 pixels (file size – 72 KB)

Uncompressed image with dimensions 75 x 56 pixels (file size – 13 KB)

Compressing Moving Images

Filmmaking, by nature, is more often concerned wi moving image. If the compression methods a described (intraframe compression) were applied to n images (a series of still frames), the end result w fifteen frames per second, it would be fine for a relatively still piece of footage, but if there was a lot of detail, such as fast movement, some may well get lost in the process. Also the audio on the film can have its quality reduced (e.g. to mono) to lower the overall file size. In addition, compression technology can be applied to the data between frames, looking for areas of redundant data.

Ultimately, whether it is intra or interframe compression that is being applied, the more you apply, the more the image quality will suffer and the greater the degree of artifacting. The first thing a filmmaker can do is to plan the film to avoid shots that will exacerbate these problems (see Chapter 12 for more information). The second thing that can be done to avoid unwanted compression is to experiment with encoding; working with it rather than against it. This is covered in more detail later on in this chapter.

The 'PEGS'

There is some discussion of the main MPEG (Moving Picture Experts Group) standards in Chapter 2; suffice to say that the influence of this group on commonly encountered compression technologies, from MP3 music files to MPEG video, is keenly felt throughout the internet.

Media Players

There are a wide variety of media players currently in circulation including Real Networks, QuickTime (Apple) and Windows Media Player (Microsoft). In order to view films on these players the films need to be made into an appropriate form for that player e.g. .rm (Real Networks), .mov (QuickTime), .wmv (Windows Media Player). (See Chapter 2 for a fuller discussion about media players and links to find out more.) This chapter contains an introduction to some of the factors that are worth considering during the encoding process, the importance of which can be demonstrated by following the encoding process described below.

Encoding Your Film

After you have decided what format you want to make your web film in, you then have two choices. You can use encoding software that has been provided by the manufacturer of the player, such as QuickTime Pro, or use post-production software such as Final Cut Pro or Premiere.[8] In Appendix V we provide an example of encoding using QuickTime Pro 5, which will result in films made in one specific format – .mov. The latter examples are able to produce films in a variety of different file formats. As this area is so vast, the only way to determine which encoding software is best for you is through trial and error, and will be largely dependant on what software is available to you at the time. Many of the software packages that you can use to encode films will have a wizard that will guide you through the encoding process, but we include a few pointers worth understanding so that you have some control over the final result.[9] All of the parameters discussed will have an effect on the outcome of the final film; the best thing to do is just experiment and see which ones you like best.

Conclusion

In summary, compression technologies are currently an integral part of the production process when making films for the internet and it will be a far smoother process if you work with these tools rather than against them. Each separate piece of compression software or hardware will have its own unique effect upon the work you have produced. Experimenting with both the settings and types of compression that can be applied can be a painstaking process, but for the web filmmaker it is both vital and rewarding.

Links for Further Doing

MPEG Homepage
http://www.chiariglione.org/mpeg

New Media Republic website, 'What is Compression?'
http://newmediarepublic.com/dvideo/compression/adv04.html

plugincinema's forum to discuss your ideas and practices
http://www.plugincinema.com/plugin/forum

References and Notes

1 See Chapter 11 for more information on the process at work in transporting files over the internet.

2 For more on Run Length Encoding see the excellent New Media Republic website
http://www.newmediarepublic.com/dvideo/compression/adv05.html

3 For more information on Winzip see http://www.winzip.com and for more information on Ultimate Zip see
http://www.ultimatezip.com

4 The code used to compress it could easily be cracked, but that's another story!

5 For more on Intraframe compression see the New Media Republic website
http://www.newmediarepublic.com/dvideo/compression/adv06.html

6 Or 'color' if you are reading this in the US of A!

7 For more on Interframe compression see the New Media Republic website
http://www.newmediarepublic.com/dvideo/compression/adv07.html

8 Final Cut Pro is produced by Apple and more information on it can be found here – **http://www.apple.com/finalcutpro** and Premiere is produced by Adobe and more information on it can be found here **http://www.adobe.com/products/premiere/main.html**

9 A 'wizard' is the name given to a step-by-step dialogue box intended to guide the user though a process in an easier manner.

Chapter 11: Using the Internet as a Cinema

Starting at the Beginning

This chapter looks at the various ways a film can be shown and distributed using the internet. Before we get down to details, it is worth taking a moment to remind ourselves how the internet works. To start with, take the basic definition of the internet as a collection of millions of computers, all of which have the potential to share information or receive data using the same universal 'language' known as Transmission Control Protocol/Internet Protocol (TCP/IP).[1]

Websites and Servers

This language (TCP/IP) is used to form a network that allows computers accessing the internet to find specific locations. One specific location that most people access frequently on the internet is a website. A website is a set 'address', where information is stored frequently in a form that can be accessed using the TCP/IP protocols. As all information on the internet ultimately derives from computers talking to one another, these websites need to be accessible twenty-four hours a day, seven days a week. It is also important that the information is stored on a computer that is set up to meet these exacting demands. A computer set up in this manner is known as a 'server' (or 'webserver'). Normally servers have special software installed and are far more powerful than a home computer. Servers will also have names that allow your computer to find them across the internet, known as Uniform Resource Locators (URL), web addresses or domain names (for example www.plugincinema.com). Using the TCP/IP protocol, your computer connects to the server that is storing the website (also known as 'hosting') and begins receiving whatever information you have requested.

The Stateless Approach

Most websites consist of text and graphics only. This content is reasonably small (in terms of file size) and is therefore easy to transport over the internet. To give an example of the file size for text, this entire book could easily be stored in 700,000 bytes and fit on a single floppy disk. Images are slightly larger; for example, just the plugincinema logo takes up 80,000 bytes of storage space.[2] However, most images found on the internet are compressed (see Chapter 10) and so occupy a relatively small amount of space.

When your computer connects to a website, the text and graphical information is sent using what is known as the 'stateless approach'. This is where the server hosting the website pushes the information to your computer as fast as possible and once done, disconnects you, in order to make itself ready to deal with other requests for data. The stateless approach means that you will not see the website or image until the server has pushed the entire body of the text or image over to your computer (there are a few exceptions, but they would add unnecessary confusion at this point[3]). This approach works fine with smaller files sizes.

The Streaming Approach

Audio, video and other rich media file types are by their very nature significantly larger. For example, the RealNetworks media version of the plugincinema film *George the Mewvie* is still over 800,000 bytes in size, despite being heavily compressed.[4] If you were required to wait until the whole file had been received from the server, then you would be waiting a long time. To attempt to remedy this problem, a new approach to transferring video and audio files was required – we will call it the 'streaming approach'. The streaming approach enables the user to access a section of the file before the entire file has been downloaded. While the user is viewing this section of the file, more data will be downloaded, waiting to be displayed (or listened to) straight after the existing section has finished. The process of downloading a portion of streamed data ready for use is known as 'buffering'. If working correctly, when a user clicks on a 'streaming' file she or he will not notice the downloading, apart from a small delay at the beginning while the file 'buffers' and the media player loads.

Using this approach, a file that consists of several minutes of compressed video, now only requires a short delay before a viewer is able to see a particular film. The streaming approach means that video and audio files are now easily accessible to all web-users.

There are two forms of media streaming: live and pre-recorded. Live media streaming is also referred to as 'webcasting'. (It should be noted that the term webcasting is also used to refer to other visual/audio transmissions of data such as video-conferencing and power point presentations.) Webcasting requires the use of specialist software such as Peercast[5] or a specialist service such as Webcast2000.[6] Live streaming is used for live broadcasts and as it is of limited value to the web filmmaker, it is therefore not covered in this book.

Pre-recorded media streaming involves preparing media files into a web-ready format. The user can then visit the website hosting the file and view it using the streaming approach. The user need do no more than acquire a compatible media player (see Chapter 2) and click on the relevant link. To facilitate this, web filmmakers need to encode films into the appropriate format.

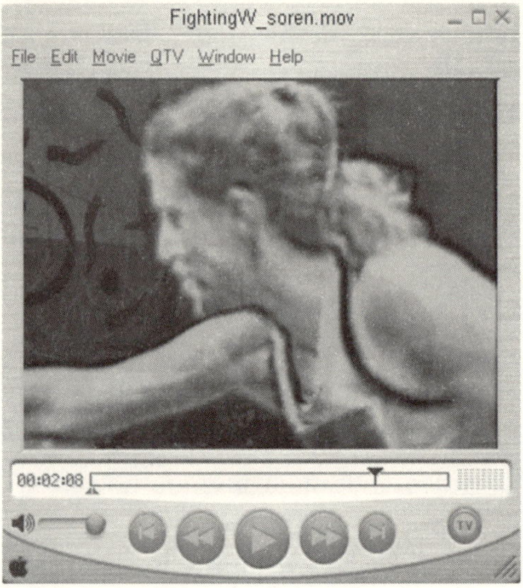

***Fighting Women II*, Dir. Ana Kronschnabl, 2002**

Hosting Your Own

If you have decided that you wish to use your own server (or use a portion of a server, known as a 'virtual server') to host your films, the most common method is to rent server space from an existing hosting company (for guidance see www.findmyhost.com for the US and www.findyourhost.co.uk for the UK). As it is both a technically and logistically complex task to set up and run your own server, this section will examine the simplest option: renting.[7]

Having your own server space means you can host what you like, when you like, subject to the restrictions imposed by the hosting company. When you rent space on a server, you never physically see the machine; all the processing is handled remotely over the internet. The server can also be sited in any country in the world (where an internet connection exists); its geographic location has no bearing on the accessibility afforded to you or any other user. There are a number of other factors, however, that you will need to consider when deciding on a hosting company:

Storage Space How much do the various hosting companies provide and is it enough for your needs? To give an idea of the space that would be needed, the twenty second long film *Tuned* which can be found on plugincinema, if stored as a .avi, encoded using the DivX OpenCodec (see Appendix IV), takes up 1.5 MB of space.[8] (The file format .avi, or Audio Visual Interleaved, is a film file format that is commonly used to store such content. It is defined as being a format that adheres to the Microsoft Windows Resource Interchange File Format (RIFF) and is commonly, though not exclusively, found on Microsoft Windows machines. Without additional compression (such as that applied in Appendix IV and V) this format can result in large data files and so becomes unwieldy for distributing films on the internet.)

Bandwidth This is the amount of data that can be accessed from your server within a set period of time. This needs to be examined carefully, as it has a bearing on the number of people able to download information from your site at a specific time, and as many hosting companies provide differing bandwidth usage depending on whether you are hosting rich-media content or just plain text. Look into the charges that apply if you do exceed the limits imposed and should your film become popular, ensure that you understand the implications[9] (you do not, for example, want to be landed with huge bills you cannot meet just as your site or film really starts to take off). Fortunately, there are guides online that can help you calculate the relevant information.[10] To give some idea of this, the average bandwidth taken by all films hosted on plugincinema (as of April 2004) is around 35 MB per day. This represents the viewing of about ten films a day in a variety of sizes and formats.

Technical Support How is the technical support provided (via email, chat room or telephone?) and, if the hosting company is not in your country, how expensive is this support to access? The best possible service you are looking for is support that is free! Even a host in another company may offer support via email or 'online-chat'; this means that you don't have to pay for long distance calls to solve your problems.

Server Software Most hosting companies offer a choice of software that is running on the server such as Unix, Linux or Windows and it is essential that you make sure this software is compatible with the films you plan to host. For example, some Linux server software packages will not allow Windows Media Player files to stream. Also look for additional options such as Streaming Server support (see below).

Total Costs Make sure you check out all the various costs: set-up fees, monthly fees, hidden costs and optional extras such as additional fees to set up chat rooms, provide detailed statistics of your site users, add a shop system or secure credit card information.

TP Also known as File Transfer Protocol, this is a process that allows you to transfer files to and from your server with a software program known as an FTP client. These can often be downloaded free of charge.[11]

Third Party Hosting

There are a number of companies and websites that will provide either space for your own website or show your films online (one such site is plugincinema.com). Some provide these services for free but some may charge, so assess the service being offered by the sites carefully. Do not be fooled into paying for a service by talk of links to 'the industry'; there are plenty of websites that will help for free if that is what you really want. Providers of free websites often have tight limits on how much space and bandwidth will be offered but this should not stop the enterprising web filmmaker from taking advantage of their generosity. In the links section at the end of this chapter, you can find more information on how to choose the company best suited to your needs.

Streaming Servers

A streaming server is one with software installed to enhance the streaming process. This does not mean that in order to stream a media file you must have a streaming server, but if you do have one the streaming will be faster and more efficient. Many of the major software companies produce their own brand of streaming server software. Microsoft offers the Windows Media Services 9 Series, as part of the Windows Server 2003,[12] and Apple's version, the QuickTime Streaming Server, claims to deliver both QuickTime and MPEG-4 files as well as having the capacity for both live and pre-recorded media.[13] It is also interesting to note that Apple has made their streaming server source-code freely available as part of their foray into Open Source (see Chapter 3 for more info)[14] and there are various other Open Source software systems such as MPEG4IP.[15] RealNetworks has the Helix Universal server, which the company claims, 'can deliver over 10,000 concurrent audio streams on standard hardware.'[16]

Setting up and maintaining a streaming server requires a degree of technical understanding and is too complex to explain in this book. However, if you wish to explore how to do this yourself, see link for 'Further Doing' at the end of this chapter.

Websites

Once you have obtained server space, you can start to build yourself a website as the base from which to launch your film. You still need to design a site, even if your ultimate goal is just to show films, and if you have never done this before a possible starting point is to explore Hyper Text Mark-up Language (HTML). For a tutorial on how to make a basic webpage using HTML, see Appendix VI. Most websites are built using HTML and if you know a little of this scripting language you can easily build a basic site. Do not be put off by the apparent complexity of HTML, it's much simpler than it looks and there are many sites offering free tutorials that will teach you the code you need to build a basic website. The advantages of learning HTML are many: you will gain greater understanding of the technological environment in which you operate and there is no need to purchase special software as it can all be done in freely available text editors such as Notepad. Even if you do choose to obtain specific web design software it's still important to understand the basics of HTML because if anything goes wrong, you'll need to be able to fix it (and it will!)[17] For more information on HTML and making a webpage, see Appendix VI.

Peer-to-Peer Distribution

Peer-to-peer networks offer an alternative method of distribution that does not require a server or website. This approach was touched upon in Chapter 4, when we discussed digital broadcasters Pseudo and their plan for a one hour show which was to be made available though the Kazaa peer-to-peer network. Your work can be distributed in the same manner: you simply sign your computer up to a peer-to-peer network. (See Chapter 1 for more information on how peer-to-peer/file trade networks operate.)

To distribute your work using this method you will first

need access to an internet connection. You will then need to download and install some peer-to-peer network software (such as Gnutella or Kazaa) and place your work in the shared directory on your PC.[18] Whenever your computer is connected to the network other people are able to copy your work onto their PC, and of course, as more people copy your work it becomes available in more places and the more other users can access it. This system works as a positive feedback loop; the more people copy your work, the more people are able to copy your work. For a tutorial on how to make an OpenCodec film and distribute it using Gnutella, see Appendix VI.

Initially, your PC will be the only place (or 'node') where users can access the work in question. To increase this you will need to spread the word, enticing people who may be interested in your work to take a copy. This is where a website may help, giving people the details of your work, which peer-to-peer network you are using and suggested times at which your PC will be switched on for interested users to take a copy. You can also use relevant bulletin boards (online notice boards) and mailing lists, in order to circulate this information.

It is important to consider how someone will search for your file when using a peer-to-peer network:[19]

Filename This will affect the search and is what the users will see, so make it appropriate and interesting. If the filename is Test_Film_B.mov this tells a user nothing about its content. However, if it was called The_Lost_Jedi_A_Star_Wars_Drama.mov you can see how the user might be enticed to copy and watch it. For clarity, it is recommended that you use an underscore _ and not a space to separate words and it is advisable to keep filenames short (less than forty characters).

Movie Information This is added to an encoded film to provide additional information, and you should keep in mind the fact that some peer-to-peer networks search for this data. (See Chapter 10 for more info.)

Since late 2003/early 2004 the news has been filled with the ongoing saga of the Recording Association of America's legal battle against ordinary users of file trade networks.[20] This chapter of the saga began in September 2003, when the first wave of 250 lawsuits against individual users was launched by the RIAA.[21] A significant cross-section of American society was being sued, as Wired.com reported: 'The defendants include a working mom, a college football player and a 71-year-old grandpa.' [22]
It is legitimate, therefore, to wonder whether the method of distribution outlined above is legal? The answer depends on what you are distributing, regardless of whether you consider your work to be copyright, copyleft or anticopyright. If your work contains copyrighted material and you are not within the 'Fair Use' laws then it is not legal (see Chapter 3). However, using a peer-to-peer network to access non-copyrighted material or material that the creator has given permission to copy, is perfectly legal in most countries.[23]

Important: It is strongly recommended that you take the time to ensure your computer is protected by anti-virus software, a firewall and by checking regularly with the manufacturers of your operating system for security updates. (A firewall is a software package designed to protect your computer from any attempts at unauthorised accesses.)[24]

Conclusion

Lev Manovich, Associate Professor at the Visual Arts Department in the University of California and author of the highly regarded *The Language of New Media,* offered this cautionary note on the distribution of web films, '...broadband is arriving much more slowly than people expected. In addition, the shift away from desktop computers towards cell phones, PDAs[25] and similar small electronic devices as the new "hub" of communication and gateway to the internet is not necessarily a good thing for online filmmaking. Yes, atomfilms.com distributes films for PDAs, but how many people watch them?'[26] This is a cautionary tale: without the correct approach to distributing your work, much of your effort will be squandered. Some of the methods discussed are complex and will require more research on your part yet make no mistake about it, the internet offers an unprecedented opportunity for global distribution that has never existed before – but only to those who take the time and trouble to understand it.

Links for Further Doing

Apple's guide to server bandwidth
http://docs.info.apple.com/article.html?artnum=24937

Apple's open source streaming server project
http://developer.apple.com/darwin/projects/streaming

FTP Software – WS_FTP
http://www.ftpplanet.com/download.htm

FTP Software on thefreesite.com
http://www.thefreesite.com/Free_Software/FTP_freeware

Gnutella
http://www.gnutella.com (NB: To connect to the Gnutella network you will need to select a 'client'. This is the software system you will be using to access the network. We use Gnucleus as a client. Ssee **http://www.gnutella.com/connect** and **http://www.gnucleus.com/Gnucleus** for more info.)

'Hosting Your Own' on Find My Host (US)
http://www.findmyhost.com

'Hosting Your Own' on Find Your Host (UK)
http://www.findyourhost.co.uk

'Free Hosting With Others' Lycos Angelfire
http://angelfire.lycos.com

'Free Hosting With Others' Yahoo! Geocities
http://geocities.com

HTML Basics Tutorial
http://www.w3schools.com/html/html_intro.asp

Kazaa
http://www.kazaa.com

Opendivx – Free Codec for Films
http://www.projectmayo.com

plugincinema.com 'Guide to lo-fi film distribution'
http://www.plugincinema.com/plugin/articles/lofi.htm

plugincinema.com's film submission guide
http://www.plugincinema.com/plugin/plugin_cinema/submit.htm

plugincinema.com & Camcorder User's 'In-depth Guide to Streaming'
http://www.plugincinema.com/plugin/film_school/streaming1.htm

RealNetworks' Streaming Media FAQ
http://www.realnetworks.com/resources/startingout/get_started_faq.html

References and Notes

1 The website of UC Berkeley Library has a good guide to the internet and how it works
http://www.lib.berkeley.edu/TeachingLib/Guides/Internet/WhatIs.html

2 For plugincinema logos see the following page
http://www.plugincinema.com/plugin/about_us/pressimages.htm

3 For example there is an Interlaced GIF which loads progressively, but this type of data is more the exception that the rule. The following site has more on interlaced GIFs
http://www.webstyleguide.com/graphics/gifs.html

4 To see the film in question
http://www.plugincinema.com/plugin/plugin_cinema/index.htm#f26

5 http://www.peercast.org

6 http://www.webcast2000.com

7 Philip Greenspun's site has information on how to set up a server http://philip.greenspun.com/panda/server.html

8 For *Tuned* see http://www.plugincinema.com/plugin/plugin_cinema/index.htm#f16

9 A sudden surge of interest in a website or file is known as the 'slashdot effect'. For more info see http://slashdot.org/faq/slashmeta.shtml

10 Apple's website includes information on calculating bandwidth usage http://docs.info.apple.com/article.html?artnum+24937

11 Use this link to find free FTP software. Check the license agreements on any software you wish to use first! http://www.ftpplanet.com/download.htm

12 http://www.microsoft.com/windows/windowsmedia/9series/server.aspx

13 http://www.apple.com/quicktime/products/qtss/qtssfaq.html

14 As opposed to free software (by this we mean free as in cost free, not free as in the Free Software Foundation!), the advantage of software that you pay for tends to be that it is more advanced and so less prone to problems. It is also likely to have more features and options and would ordinarily receive a certain level of support provided free of charge by the manufacturer. For the Apple streaming server software see http://developer.apple.com/darwin/projects/streaming.

15 http://mpeg4ip.net

16 http://www.realnetworks.com/products/server

17 Examples of web design software include: Dreamweaver see http://www.macromedia.com/software/dreamweaver and FrontPage see http://www.microsoft.com/frontpage and Quanta see http://quanta.sourceforge.net

18 Peer-to-peer software has a directory known as the 'shared files' directory, from which network users are allowed access your

files. See the 'Gnutella Frequently Asked Questions' (FAQ) on koeln.ccc.de for more on this http://koeln.ccc.de/archiv/hackschiffseiten/information/faq.html

19 There is a presentation entitled 'Gnutella, Freenet and Peer to Peer Networks' by Norman Eng, Steven Hnatko & George Papadopoulos which has much more detail about how such systems operate and how the searches work. (To read this document try downloading the file and use a program such as Open Office to view.) http://ipsit.bu.edu/sc546/546projects/hnatko/Gnutella,%20Freenet%20and%20Peer%20to%20Peer%20Networks.ppt

20 See the plugincinema news archive for more information on this news story http://www.plugincinema.com/plugin/newsarchive/news092003.htm

21 http://www.wired.com/news/digiwood/0,1412,60345,00.html

22 http://www.wired.com/news/digiwood/0,1412,60366,00.html

23 This site, produced in association with the Recording Industry Association of America has the US based legal information on this point http://www.musicunited.org/2_thelaw.html#5

24 You can get a free firewall from ZoneAlarm. See http://www.zonelabs.com but made sure you check the license agreements on any software you wish to use first! Ensure also that you take the time to ask whether the manufacturer you opt for offers help and support. Does the program run on your operating system and to the specifications of your computer? Does the purchase price offer a period (often one year or so) during which the manufacturers will offer updates for the software to keep it abreast of developments in hacking and virus technology? See the following article for more information http://www.cert.org/homeusers/HomeComputerSecurity

25 PDA or Personal Digital Assistant is a tiny portable PC that offers much of the staple functionality of a computer, such as an address book, email system, diary, calculator and so on.

Increasingly, they are being used to deliver entertainment too; including games, films and music.

26 To read the full text of the interview see http://www.plugincinema.com/plugin/plugin_aesthetic/levmanovich.htm

Chapter 12: A Practical Manifesto

Bringing the Manifesto to Life!

In Chapter 5 we introduced the pluginmanifesto but for the ideas it champions to have any enduring meaning they need to be applicable to real-life filmmaking! In this chapter we will take a closer look at how some of these ideas can guide filmmakers on a practical level as well as examining how some of these ideas can be applied in their own filmmaking practice.

A film made for viewing on the internet is not 1_hours long.

This point arises from the various technical issues surrounding the distribution of a long film. With current technology, a long film means large file sizes and a large file size involves a number of important practical considerations:

- Larger files take up more space on a server. This is an important consideration as there may be restricted bandwidth usage from the provider hosting your films (see Chapter 11). It also has implications for the amount of people able to view the film at the same time, as the greater the file size, the less people can view the file. With file size, small is beautiful!
- Another inherent danger of the internet of large files is 'timeout'. A timeout happens during the process of transferring data or maintaining a connection, when a program is left waiting for the next bit of information for so long that the entire process is re-set. There is a good chance that if someone is streaming an hour-long film it will timeout, with the consequence that the viewer has to re-log onto the site, resulting in an interrupted and unnecessarily complicated viewing experience.

It does not have to have a narrative – structure can come from a variety of means...

At this point, it is worth reminding ourselves that the viewing platform we are discussing is a computer and not a TV set or cinema screen. Whilst this can create complications, it also provides more creative possibilities in terms of content since computers are a more interactive delivery platform. In addition, the networking and constant progression of technology means that filmmaking for the internet is constantly evolving:

- The story itself can be made interactive, with the interactive elements of the internet enabling the filmmaker to explore narrative in new ways. One such (more text based) interactive narrative created by digital artist Mark Amerika and entitled *Grammatron*, is an interactive story loosely based on the myth of the golem (a creature allegedly created from magic and earth). In an interview for plugincinema, Mark remarked on the similarities of his work to film, '...I can totally see *Grammatron* as early desktop cinema. It has all the ingredients of multi-media, multi-linear storytelling and is made in the tradition of filmmakers like Vertov, Godard and Marker.'
- Films do not have to be shown in their entirety, they could be broken down into smaller episodes that the audience can follow by logging on periodically. This is an alternative method of managing a longer plotline, especially considering the previous points made. One ambitious example of this type of episodic production was the online film series *NewBlood* 'a stylish thriller set in contemporary London's clubland and bar culture.' This idea can be further explored by incorporating audience feedback into the plotline. An example of this is the BBC

Radio 4 drama *The Dark House*, where the online component allowed users to choose which character related the narrative and then to share their choice with other listeners.

Forget Hollywood...film can be art!

This statement is intended to urge filmmakers to view their work from angles other than the traditional perspectives. This is vital for innovation and change, but will only happen once practitioners start taking the filmmaking process apart and working with the technology to find new ways to reassemble it all – the innovations of today are the accepted methods of tomorrow. As inconceivable as it may seem given the current content of films available on general release today, one of the first films ever made actually scared its audience with a simple shot of a train pulling into the station. Filmmaking has moved on since 1895, however, and many of the advances that have been made involved the discovery of new techniques for storytelling, whether that was shot-reverse-shot editing (establishing a link between two things in separate shots by placing the shots next to each other) or compressing time (this is often done by showing a character embarking on an action and then showing them finishing it: the audience naturally fills in the gap between). Below are a few aspects of the internet that can be used to innovate beyond Hollywood:

Immediacy There can be an instantaneous quality to the web filmmaking process that traditional film production methods, with their beaurocracy and physical distribution limitations, cannot compete with. A good example of this immediate technology in practice is the Indymedia movement. This is a global network of news websites that allow anyone to upload their own writing, audio or video content, which is then instantly accessible by others to read, listen or view.[8]

'Bottom-Up' Filmmaking Hollywood is notoriously hierarchical and top-down in its production processes.[9] However, by encouraging feedback and seeing your film as an ongoing creative process you can engage with the audience and so react to their views and ideas on your work. Either through email, online forms or bulletin boards, it is easy for a filmmaker to encourage people to provide a response to their work. This feedback can then be fed back into the project to allow it to evolve even further. This idea can also be linked with the principals of copyleft/anticopyright (see Chapter 3) to not only encourage feedback, but to encourage audiences to take your work and act on the feedback themselves!

Co-operative Filmmaking The internet is a powerful communications medium; so let's communicate! Filmmakers can take advantage of the ease with which they can contact others and work with them on various projects despite the limitations of geography, as information such as text, images and footage can easily be transferred. One such example of this concept in action is the recently opened Guerrilla News Network 'Media Traders' forum which encourages filmmakers to get together: 'Need that missing element for your own guerrilla media making? Have media or skills you are willing to share? Post requests and offers for video clips, photos, graphics, music, etc. and collaborate with your fellow guerrillas.'

Limitations can be creative – if you do not have a wind machine, use a fan. If you do not have the bandwidth, do not expect the cinema.

It is always worth remembering that limitation can be a

creative force, or as the old saying goes: 'Necessity is the mother of invention.'

- One of the most well known successes in filmmaking who espouses the creativity of working within limitations is Robert Rodriguez (as mentioned in Chapter 8), director of *Desperado* and *From Dusk Till Dawn*. In his '10 Minute Film School' he remarks: 'When I did *El Mariachi* I had a turtle, I had a guitar case, I had a small town and I said I'll make a movie around that.' And the proof of this method? Look no further than the critically acclaimed *Desperado* – it was made for the tiny (by Hollywood standards!) budget of $7 million but has grossed over $26 million so far.
- Another good example of limitations being used in a positive manner is the film *Cube*, directed by Vincenzo Natali and written by Natali, Andre Bijelic and Graeme Manson. This sci-fi thriller tells the story of six people who one day awake to find they are imprisoned in a deadly maze. The film was made by re-dressing the same room over and over, creating feelings of claustrophobia and familiarity but had the important side-effects of keeping production costs very, very low.

Use Codecs and compression creatively.

Compression is currently a reality of internet technology and is likely to remain so for some time to come. If you believe that you do not need to be concerned about compression with the arrival of broadband and other forms of high-speed access – think again! In the December 2002 Nielsen/Netratings survey of US internet users, only 31% had access to a high-speed or broadband connection and whilst this figure is continually increasing, operating from a start point that cuts out 69% of your audience is hardly advisable. Secondly, even aiming at the broadband audience will involve some form of compression. So, our advice is to go with the technology, do not fight it! (A fuller discussion of compression can be found in Chapter 10.) The types of shots and techniques used in traditional filmmaking are discussed below in relation to their implications for web filmmaking. The following are loose definitions of the shot styles and their internet equivalents:

Types of Shot

Close Up and Extreme Close Up

This shot – a close-up – is used by a filmmaker to pick out the details and/or actions that are important to the narrative. Most often it is used to show expressions on faces or important objects within the story such as a key or gun. An extreme close-up is, as the name suggests, a more extreme version of the close-up and will focus in on the subject of the shot to an even greater extent.

For the web filmmaker, close-ups look good as the action or object is larger within the frame and therefore clearer. This is a good choice of shot but one note of caution must be sounded – close-ups that involve the audience having to read writing or understand the significance of other similar fine details must be filmed extremely carefully as heavy compression can 'smudge' out such details.

Long Shot/Extreme Long Shot

A long shot shows events, actions or a landscape from a distance. It can often be seen in films being used as an establishing shot; an opening view into a scene that places the narrative in a definite and recognizable location. An extreme long shot places the subject of the shot at an even greater distance and is often used to further enhance a sense of isolation or a particular location.

For the web filmmaker, compression can dampen the effect of this shot, especially at extreme ranges. For example, if your shot shows figures running along a hilltop, the compression could blur the figures until it is difficult to identify the events that are transpiring.

Medium Shot

A common shot, this can be defined as a view at the mid-point between the long shot and a close up. It is often used for conversations in film and TV where it would typically frame two or three people having a conversation.

For the web filmmaker it is important not to overload the framing of the shot with too many figures or events. This way the main areas of the shot will undergo less compression thus retaining the essential information.

Pan

This is a shot in which the the camera follows a horizontal movement path, moving from side to side, pivoting from a fixed point. This shot is primarily used to follow an action, for example, a figure walking along a street.
Particular consideration should be given to the effect of compression upon this type of shot, as artifacting, which involves the blurred or pixilated patches appearing in an image where the compression technology has resulted in a noticeable loss of quality, is most apparent when there is a greater difference between the contents of each frame. If every area of the frame changes dramatically as the camera moves it will result in considerable artifacting.

Tracking/Dolly Shot

This shot is similar to a pan shot in that the camera follows the action, except that here the camera itself moves. For the web filmmaker the issues here are similar to those found with the pan shot, see above.

Filmmakers and geeks should be friends.

Often the greatest innovations come from a merging of the creative and technical mindset. To achieve this, the artificial walls that are often erected around the technical aspects of production and the creative aspects must be dismantled; after all, the movement that is so dramatically changing the music business did not come from a singer, popstar or music executive – it came from a programmer (see Chapter 1). Working with people from differing disciplines and with different sets of skills to your own can often yield fresh and inspiring results for all parties concerned.

- Take inspiration from the old-skool! An impressive champion of the experimental usc of technology is the photographic pioneer Eadweard Muybridge. In the late 1800s he was experimenting with a technique that would allow him to photograph movement with a 'stills' camera. To capture the nuances of mammalian movement, he developed a technique using 12 stereoscopic cameras in a 50 foot long shed. The subject of his photographs would run down a path, along which were set up multiple trip wires, linked to multiple cameras. As the subject moved, their progress triggered the cameras, thereby capturing the subtleties of their movement. The idea of using a huge number of cameras focused on the same subject was replicated, in a fashion, by 'bullet time'. Instead of the image being captured in sequence, each camera was triggered simultaneously, resulting in a pausing of the subject in time but not in space.

  It is with this example that history comes full circle, and is how the much talked about 'Bullet Time' technique popularised in the 1999 film *The Matrix* can be seen as an evolution of Muybridge's ideas.

- Take inspiration from the nu-skool! Arguably the most visible and advanced meeting point between filmmakers and geeks is Machinima. Machinima is where the technology used to create a 3D computer game is re-used as a virtual studio to create films. Here the technology created and modified by programmers meets the ideas and practices of filmmaking to create narratives totally within a virtual realm. Hugh Hancock, Chair of Machinima

> filmmaking group, Strange Company, in an interview with plugincinema remarked, 'There's a lot of people out there putting a lot of effort into making film after film, and if you watch those films, you can't help feeling the massive potential there…That potential is breaking out, and has been for some time, into truly brilliant work, and it's going to do so more and more over the next few years.'

***Machinima: Skate Dreams*, Dir. Ana Kronschnabl, 2001 (QuickTime)**

The practicalities of filmmaking often seem far removed from the theory, however, for the web filmmaker the act of creation requires an engagement with new technology as well as older ideas. It is vital that this new and exciting form of filmmaking carves a new path both theoretically and practically. However you approach filmmaking, and whether you find the ideas here helpful or a hindrance, take the time to share your experience and ideas with other filmmakers and help evolve the art form!

Links for Further Doing

Grammatron
http://www.grammatron.com

Indymedia
http://www.indymedia.org

Muybridge's Work
http://web.inter.nl.net/users/anima/chronoph/muybridge/index.htm

plugincinema's '5 Minute Guide to Machinima Film Making' and plugincinema's 'Guide to Interactive Movie Design'
http://www.plugincinema.com/plugin/film_school/interactivemovie.htm

plugincinema's forums to discuss your ideas and practices
http://www.plugincinema.com/plugin/forum

References and Notes

1 For more on timeouts see the Newbies Corner on #HACK_YOU at http://hakyu.tripod.com/testpage/id10.html

2 See http://www.grammatron.com to see Mark's work.

3 For the full interview see http://www.plugincinema.com/plugin/plugin_aesthetic/\markamerika.htm

4 This quote is from news round up on b-movie.com: http://www.b-movie.com/sideshow/sideshow.php?SSID=29 though sadly the main site for the project, NewBlood.net, no longer seems to be active.

5 For more on this drama see http://www.bbc.co.uk/radio4/arts/darkhouse/index.shtml

6 This 1895 film was included in Channel 4's *100 Scariest Moments* poll http://www.channel4.com/film/newsfeatures/microsites/S/scary/results_100-91_1.html

7 You can find out more about the Indymedia movement from the world site: http://www.indymedia.org/about.php3

8 For example, the Indymedia site closest to where plugincinema is based is Bristol Indymedia. Bristol Indymedia can be found at http://www.bristol.indymedia.org

9 Adding email links to a webpage is easy, see one of the many online tutorials for more on this at http://www.accessv.com/~email/webpages/lesson7.html and there is a good tutorial for creating forms at http://www.pagetutor.com/pagetutor/forms/index.html plus info on setting up a bulletin board here: http://www.phpbb.com

10 plugincinema reported its launch in November 2003, you can see the forum at http://www.guerrillanews.com/forum/postlist.pl?Cat=&Board=Traders

11 The full text of the '10 Minute Film School' can be found on exposure.co.uk

http://www.exposure.co.uk/makers/minute.html

12 Figures from IGN.com http://filmforce.ign.com/articles/455/455681p1.html?fromint=1

13 For more on this film see the official website http://cubethemovie.com

14 http://www.nielsen-netratings.com/pr/pr_030115.pdf

15 There is a excellent website about Muybridge and his work here http://web.inter.nl.net/users/anima/chronoph/muybridge/index.h

16 A good walkthrough of how bullet time works can be found here http://cartoon.iguw.tuwien.ac.at/tom/quicktime/episode_2/matrix_bullettimewalkthru.html

17 For more information on this see plugincinema's '5 Minute Guide to Machinima Film Making' http://www.plugincinema.com/plugin/articles/article_machinima.htm

18 For the full interview with Hugh Hancock see http://www.plugincinema.com/plugin/plugin_aesthetic/hughhancock.htm

A Final Note (by Ana Kronschnabl)

It doesn't seem that long ago that I first started making films. I had started a film, drama and art degree in Reading, England – a pretty unusual sort of course at that time. I remember how exciting it was being given our first spools of Super8 film, waiting for them to come back from the developers. Then began the intricate art of editing: using a splicer, tape and a hand-cranked viewer.[1]

All of this sounds like a different age, reminiscences from a different era. The truth is that this was barely twenty years ago. So much has happened in terms of technology in that time, it hardly seems like the same medium; but it is. I still use the same skills I acquired all those years ago, and the feeling I get whilst wrapped up in editing is still the same. What has changed is the means by which I now create films. The tools I now have at my disposal far exceed my wildest dreams of twenty years ago. How could I have known the special effects that would be available to me, or the size of the cameras I would be using? Most incredible of all, who would have thought that I could do all this from a small room in my house, using my own equipment, with the potential to distribute my work to the whole of the interconnected world?

What has also changed is my approach to filmmaking. When I learnt about films all those years ago, although we learnt about independent filmmaking, I looked to Hollywood. We learnt about Chantal Ackerman and Brakhage, Kurosawa and Genet, but I remained fascinated by Gene Kelly and admired Scorcese.[2] What I learnt back then without realising it is that there is a canon of experimentation: something we could be forgiven for not knowing if we went to the cinema in the UK today. However, even though I was uninterested in experimental or art cinema at the time, it stayed with me.

When I first discovered the internet I was filled with excitement – it had incredible potential. Not only was it a distribution medium that could reach everyone with a net connection; but the nature of the internet also meant that I could distribute the work myself. The 70s dream of owning the means of production and distribution seemed just around the corner. As soon as I tried to make films, however, I found out why nobody was doing it. Two things instantly occurred to me: being a competent filmmaker wasn't enough – I also needed to understand computers. Secondly, if the internet was to fulfil its potential as a distribution medium, what exactly would a film that was made for the internet look like?

Initially, the first point was the hardest to reconcile, although ultimately it was the easiest one to overcome – I had to learn about computers and digital filmmaking. The second point is the one that really grabbed my imagination. If I had only had experience of Hollywood I would probably have decided that internet filmmaking had no potential, but being aware of other previous and current forms of filmmaking meant that I could see a way in. I felt that the promise of this medium could indeed be realized, I just needed to relearn and reassess my particular, entrenched approach to filmmaking. The rest, as they say, is history. Because there was nowhere I could show my films or discuss things with like-minded filmmakers, I set up plugincinema. That was almost five years ago now, and I still don't know what this new form will look like, but I am certainly having an awful lot of fun finding out.

References and Notes

1 For those of you who don't remember these bygone days, making Super8 films involved cutting the celluloid into pieces and then sticking it back together again in the order you

wanted. The need for a good storyboard becomes apparent at this stage, there are only so many times you can pull your film apart and put it back together again without ruining it.

2 Chantal Ackerman is a Belgium born independent filmmaker, I recommend the film *Toute Une Nuit* (1982). See http://www.worldartists.com/chantal.htm. Stan Brakhage is another experimental filmmaker. See http://www.phinnweb.com/links/cinemaunderground/brakhage. Akira Kurosawa is the much admired Japanese director, I recommend *The Seven Samurai* (1954). See http://home.earthlink.net/~ronintom/Kurosawa.htm. For Jean Genet I recommend *Un Chant D'Amour* (1950). For Gene Kelly, the famous Hollywood actor, choreographer and director; I recommend *Singin' in the Rain* (1952). While Martin Scorsese is better known for films like *Goodfellas* (1990), I recommend his first major film, *Who's That Knocking at My Door?* (1969).

INTRODUCTION TO APPENDICES

The following sections contain user guides on how to carry out very specific tasks. They are intended to be useful as a general guide on how to do things but using very specific equipment and with a unique outcome. It is intended to provide an overall understanding with the specifics being relevant to a particular set-up, both in terms of hardware and software.

Appendix I: A Sample Script and Storyboard
Appendix II: Capturing Digital Footage
Appendix III: Basic Editing With VirtualDubMod
Appendix IV: Distributing Films on a File Trade Network
Appendix V: Encoding Using QuickTime Pro 5
Appendix VI: Creating a Webpage for Free
Appendix VII: Using The PayPal Payment System

Appendix I: A Sample Script & Storyboard

Introduction

There is a certain amount of reluctance on our part – the team at plugincinema that is – to present script and storyboarding information as if there is only one way of doing it. In order to provide an even-handed overview this appendix will display a script and storyboard in a standardized Hollywood format as well as in a more unorthodox format. In each case, see the references and notes at the end of the chapter to find out more about the specific points of why something is laid out as it is.

Dark Star Falling

The content for this appendix is based on an unfinished script for a film entitled *Dark Star Falling* which was the work (so far) of Mark Dickenson, Darren Floyd and Tomas Rawlings. The artwork is by Stuart Griffin.

Dark Star Hollywood

The action in the next page of this appendix is written in a standard Hollywood format. On the following page, the same content will be displayed in a fairly standard storyboard format.

Dark Star Web Film

In the two pages that follow there is more of the script, but represented in a non-standard format that might be used by a web filmmaker. In this experimental layout we are using the numbered list function in a word-processor to generate the shot numbers – this means we can add and remove shots and ideas without having to re-number everything. We've also double-spaced the text, so if it is printed there is plenty of space for comments and ideas.

The storyboard takes its layout inspiration from comics – but uses the layer function found in most art packages (such as Paint Shop Pro and Photoshop) to place the comments and ideas on top of the drawings, so the space for generating ideas flows more…

Dark Star Hollywood – Script

01. INT. PUBLIC HOUSE – EARLY EVENING

PAN OF PUB

Camera pans across the pub, where we see Neil sitting at a table. The pub is a squalid dive and Neil is sitting at a small table with half a pint of flat lager in front of him and a fag smoking in the ashtray. He looks confused and disorientated. The dukebox in the corner hums an Elvis tune, 'Love me Tender', quietly in the background.

02. INT. PUBLIC HOUSE – EARLY EVENING

MEDIUM SHOT OF DOOR

A man comes in, mid-twenties wearing black jeans, black puffa jacket, flash trainers, sovereign rings and with gelled black hair.

03. INT. PUBLIC HOUSE – EARLY EVENING

LOW ANGLE TRACKING SHOT

He walks over to Neil, across the grotty floor of the pub.

The camera then moves up to end the shot from over this man's shoulder. He taps Neil on the shoulder and begins talking to him.

MAN

Ok?

MAN

(Speaks louder this time)

OK?

NEIL

Huh?

The man gives Neil a roll of cash. Absently, Neil takes this roll.

MAN

You ok mate?

NEIL

Yeah. I'm ok.

The man turns and leaves the pub.

Dark Star Hollywood – Storyboard

Shot: 01[10]

Shows inside of the pub. Camera pans over...

Shot: 01

...to show Neil sitting at a table.

Shot: 02

Unidentified man enters the pub.

Shot: 03

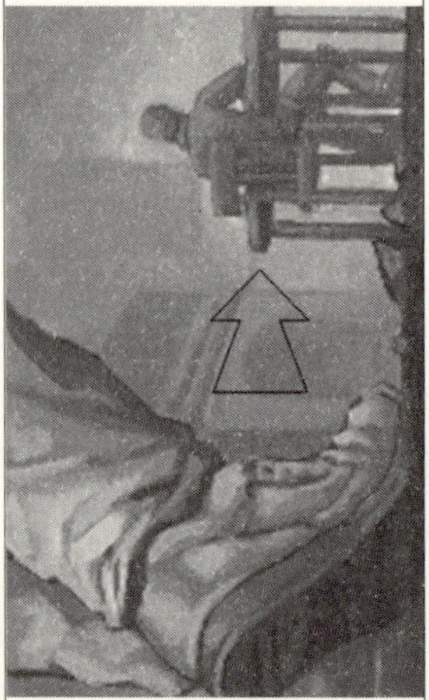

Low angle shot follows him.

Shot: 03

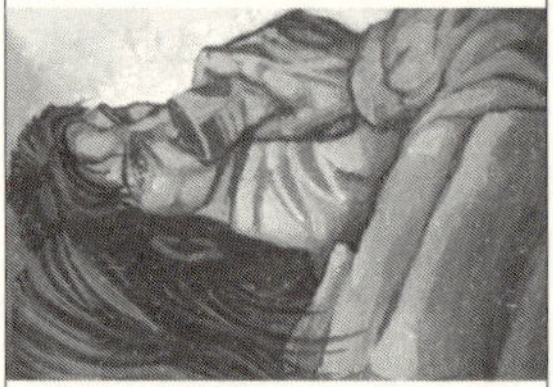

Camera pulls up to over-shoulder height.

Shot: 03

Camera swings round to show cash.

Dark Star Web film – Script

1. As the guy leaves the pub we just hear the click of footsteps…these sounds merge to…
2. …a chanting 'urch urrl ur urch urrl ur....' Neil looks over his right shoulder – this needs to be a slow look, so compression captures the turn well.

NB: This is just a made-up sound – maybe we can apply sound compression filters here to get a cool effect?

3. This figure is then shown from the front as a cut away – possibly look to Manga-like effects here with flashing background?
4. The figure (and not a 'he' because this guy is not supposed to look fully human even though he is wearing a human skin!) is chanting as he walks past Neil: 'urch urrl ur urch urrl ur...' As he passes we see a 'yelp' of surprise from Neil – even though we can't see why.
5. To show what has happened a camera cuts to a close up of the arm where we see a claw ripping the flesh and drawing blood.
6. We see the alarm on Neil's face and the pleasure on the face of the figure. Something really weird is going on!
7. The figure walks off waving goodbye as Neil, suddenly with more speed, jumps up registering the shock of what has just happened.
8. As Neil yells around the figure tastes the blood – and likes what it tastes.
9. We show the floor and the blood from the arterial wound drip…drip…dripping…onto the floor.

Dark Star Web film – Storyboard

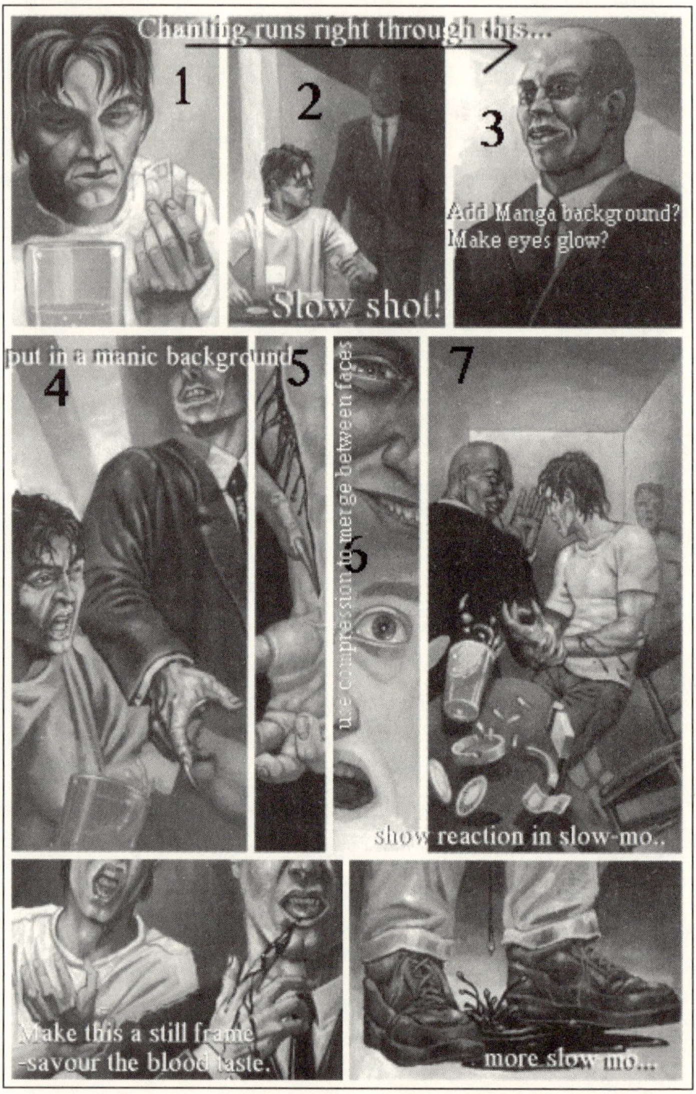

References and Notes

1 The whole script (so far) is the work of Mark Dickenson, Darren Floyd and Tomas Rawlings. It is based on an original idea by Tomas Rawlings. Conceived circa 1996. This text is based on Version 1.1, 23/08/00. This action is from Scene 3, originally written by Tomas Rawlings.

2 There are a variety of possible methods for script layout. This appendix will shoot one common method. This layout was the one used for a version of the script of the *The Great Escape* held in MGM's archives. Version from April 26, 1962 by James Clavell. For more on this see http://www.plugincinema.com/plugin/film_school/script_1.htm

3 Each time the camera is cut a new section is begun in the script. This change is given an underlined title. The number is the shot number; the title also contains the location and time of day. This is written in UPPER CASE.

4 Each scene change can also have camera view information below the title. This is written in UPPER CASE.

5 Written in lower case comes information about the shot such as what people are doing, important set directions or props involved.

6 When a character speaks, their name is written in UPPER CASE in the centre of the page.

7 The speech is indented from the edge of the page to begin further in.

8 If there are voice or stage directions that accompany this speech, then indented below the name of the character are the details (in brackets).

9 You will notice that the storyboard is a landscape rather than portrait page.

10 In this style of storyboard, each box has a place to enter the shot number (which corresponds with the script) an image of

the action and an area below to write additional comments. You will also notice that the movement of people and camera is shown by large arrows.

Appendix II: Capturing Digital Footage

Introduction

There are a huge number of both hardware and software combinations for connecting a digital camera to a computer. In order to simplify the process we will provide one example using a DV camera and DVgate Motion to capture digital video (DV). Although most computers with FireWire support will come with proprietary video capture software this example should provide a useful guide, providing general principles and ways of working.

This tutorial assumes that the reader has the following equipment:

- DV camera or DV device with appropriate FireWire (i.LINK or IEEE1394) cable.
- PC running Windows XP.
- Video Capture software.

The Connection

First things first: connect your DV camera to your computer's FireWire socket while the computer is switched off. Turn the DV camera on and switch it to VTR or Video mode. Turn your computer on. Once your computer has booted up, go into 'My Computer' and check that the DV camera is present.

If you cannot see your DV camera try disconnecting and then re-connecting the FireWire cable from the computer. With Windows XP you should hear a sound every time the FireWire cable is connected or disconnected. If you still cannot see the DV camera, try re-starting the computer and check that all cables are connected properly and working. If you are still having problems contact the equipment manufacturer for further assistance.

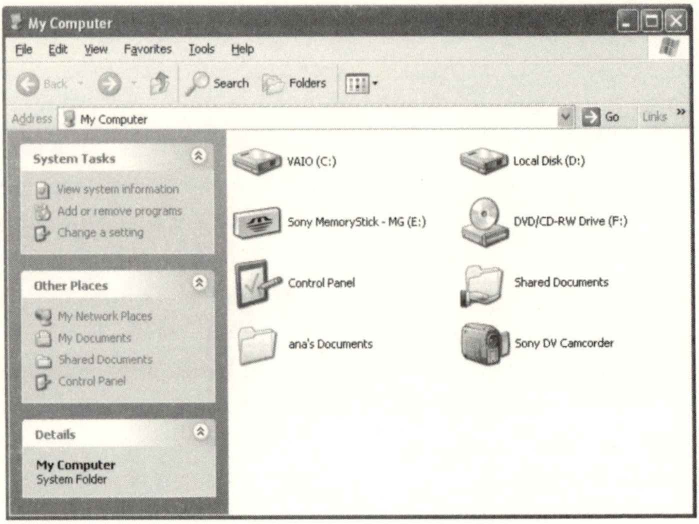

DVgate

Next open DVgate Motion, (or whatever capture software package is available to you). Make sure the DV camera is available or 'online'. This will allow you to control the DV camera from the computer.

DVgate Motion has two different modes for capturing video:

'**IMPORT - Auto**' mode lets you specify the video clips that you want to capture while viewing the playback of the DV footage in the monitor window. This can be done by selecting (or marking) the beginning frame of the video clip (or '**IN**' point) and the end frame ('**OUT**' point) to create an EDL (edit decision list) or ('**IN/OUT list**'). The specified video clips are then captured automatically; you can just sit back and let it do the work for you.

DVgate Motion has a useful scan function that will automatically search for break points on your DV tape and set them as '**IN**' and '**OUT**' points on your edit decision list.

In '**IMPORT - Manual**' mode you will have to press play

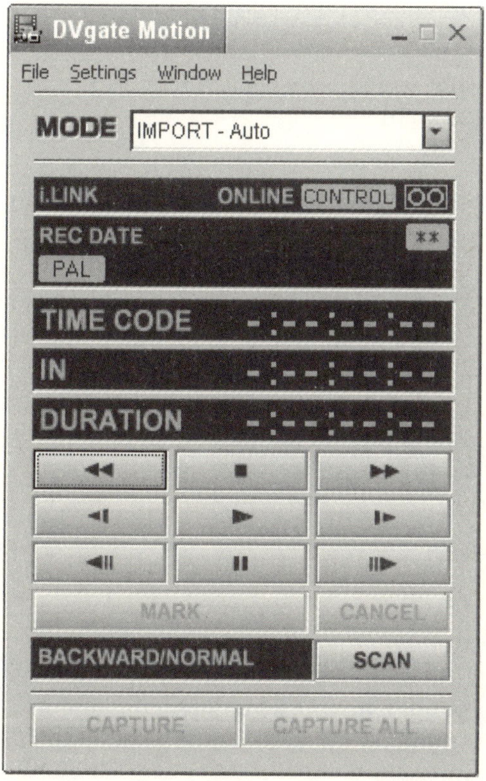

on the DV camera and capture the footage in real time. This is mainly used when the DV camera is in 'Camera' mode, or you are capturing footage from a different source such as a Digital 8 camera.

Capture Settings

When capturing DV footage you can specify the file storage format, sound type and whether to divide the files to make them more manageable. You can also capture any frames that might have been lost in the capture process.

To open the 'Capture Setting' window in DVgate Motion, select '**Settings>Capture**'.

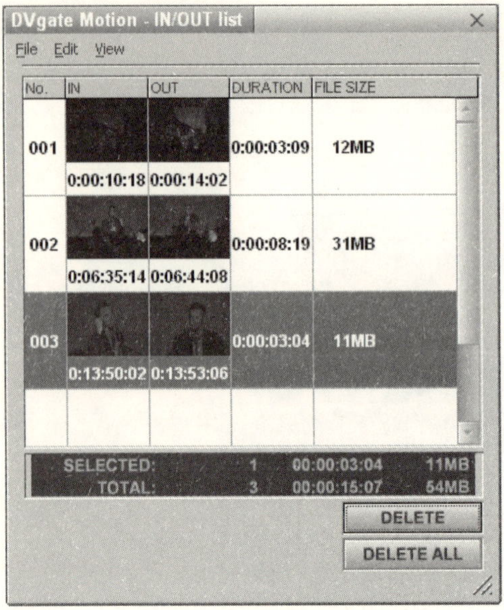

The file type available will be dependent on the DV source footage on your camera. There is also the option to record just the sound from the DV camera from the 'File type' drop-down menu.

The file can be divided either by the length of the clip or by the size of the file, both of which can be set. It is worth mentioning that the maximum duration possible for the clip is 9 minutes 30 seconds for NTSC footage, and 9 minutes 25 seconds for PAL. The file size can be specified in 1 Mbyte units. The minimum is 100 Mbytes and the maximum is 2 Gbytes (or 2048 Mbytes).

Because of this, it is likely that rather than attempting to capture all of your footage as one unwieldy file, you will opt to only capture those clips which you require to make your film.

It is worth noting that frames can be lost if the computer is not fast enough to capture DV footage, if you try to do anything else on your computer at the same time or when you are monitoring the DV footage on the computer. Selecting 'Recover Lost Frames' in the 'Capture Settings'

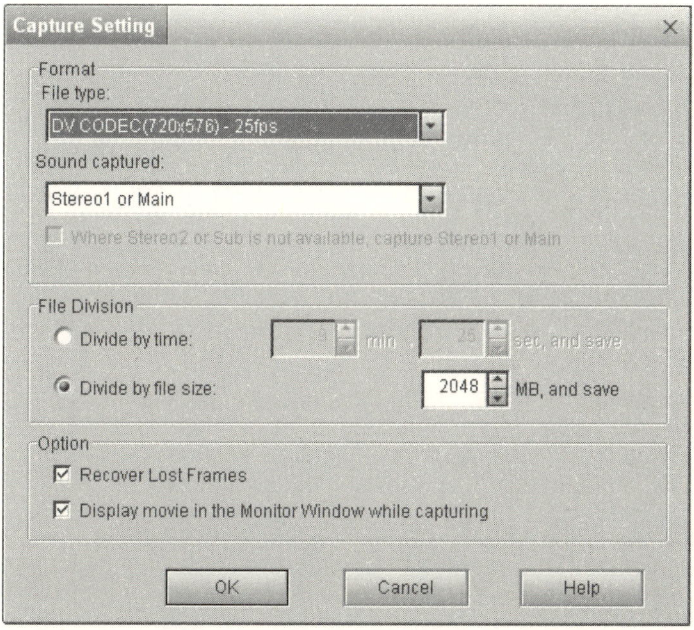

window can solve this. The number of lost frames will be displayed after the footage has been captured.

Finally...

While it is unlikely that you have the exact same camera and software as is covered above, it is hoped that this has provided you with a taste of the DV capturing process.

Appendix III: Basic Editing With VirtualDubMod

Free VirtualDubMod!

This tutorial will guide you through the basics of editing using VirtualDubMod. This piece of software is a modification (hence the name 'mod') of another editing tool called 'VirtualDub' written by Avery Lee.[1] We have chosen this particular software for the following reasons:

- It is free! This software can be downloaded free of charge, though you can donate money to the writers if you choose.[2]
- It is Free! It fits the criteria of the Free Software Foundation as the piece of software that fits with their belief in how humanity should share knowledge.
- It is small. The download is pretty small and does not need a powerful system to use, but is still offers non-linear digital editing – making it ideal to learn with.
- It is a simple, cut and paste editor with similar features to many other applications such as QuickTime Pro.[3]

For this tutorial you will need the following:

- A computer with an internet connection.
- The imported film files you have shot using a camera in an .avi file format.
- VirtualDubMod version 1.5.10.1.

In addition, if you wish to create titles and credits for your film you will also need:

- An art package that will create .tga files.[4]

- .tga files with the relevant information on.

VirtualDubMod can be found at http://virtualdubmod.sourceforge.net – hence the need for the internet connection. Once you have downloaded the correct version – locate and unzip the version of VirtualDubMod you have downloaded. This guide has been created using VirtualDubMod version 1.5.10.1 and it is suggested you use this version; this way all the instructions will exactly match those in the version you have.[5] Once downloaded from the internet it will be compressed as a .zip file (see Chapter 10 for more on this) and to unzip it you will need a piece of software such as Ultimate Zip or WinRAR.[6] If you have such a tool installed you will be able to click on the file and unzip it. On a windows machine this can be done by right-clicking on the file and selecting 'Extract to Folder'etc.

Planning the Edit

Before you start to edit, make sure you have catalogued all the footage you shot (Log Footage), made a note of which sections you wish to use and imported this material into your computer (Import/Digitize Footage). It is also recommended that you have a storyboard, so you have a plan of how the finished film will look. See Chapter 6 and 7 and Appendix I for more on all of this.

Importing and Playing Footage

First you need to get your footage into VirtualDubMod. This software can import the footage in a variety of formats, but we have made the assumption that this footage will be in the .avi format (see Appendix II).

1. Run VirtualDubMod. In Windows this is done by running the file 'VirtualDubMod.exe'.
2. Using VirtualDubMod, open your .avi file. To open

your file in VirtualDubMod, go to File>Open video file.

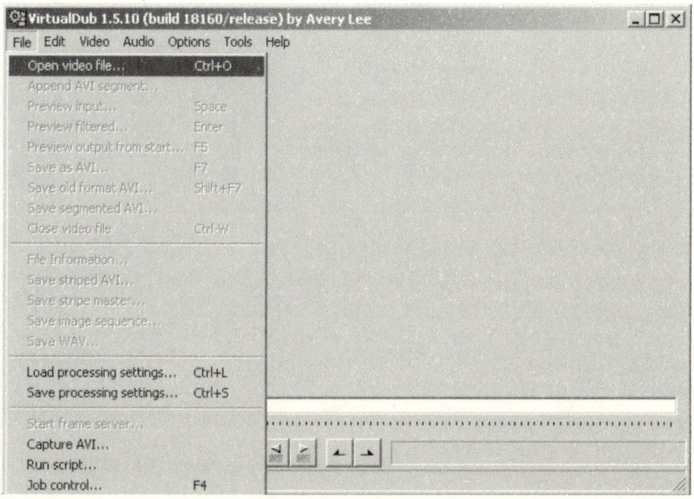

3. Try playing your footage in VirtualDubMod. This is done using the play button.

The play button, you will notice, is one of several buttons on the bottom control panel. The first seven buttons do not perform any editing functions, but they are the controls that allow you to navigate around the footage to see or get to where you wish to be. Here is a brief tour of what these buttons do:

Stop	Stops playing current footage.
Input Playback	Plays the footage you have inputted (shown in left video display).
Output Playback	Plays the footage you have altered (shown in right video display).

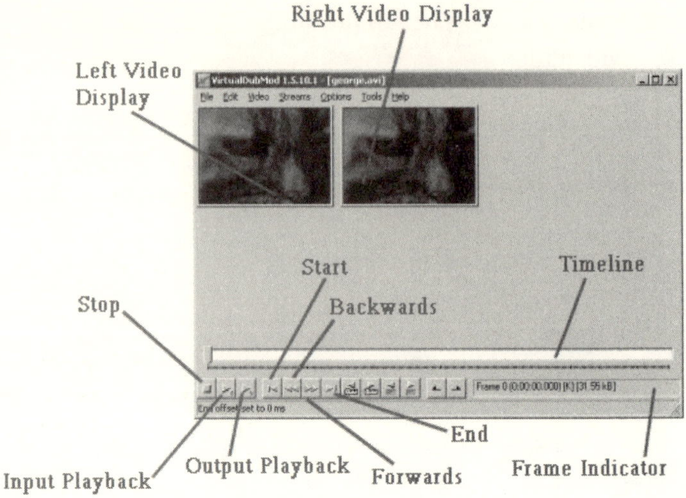

Start	Move to first frame (or the start of) the footage.
Backward	Move backwards by a single frame (to get precisely where needed).
Forward	Move forward by a single frame (allows you to get precisely where needed).
End	Move to the last frame (the end of) the footage.
Left Video Display	The area that displays the inputed footage.
Right Video Display	The area that displays the outputed footage.
Timeline	A bar representing the length of the footage.
Frame Indicator	Tells you what the current frame number you are looking at is.

Cutting and Pasting

This is the most basic process, and the building block of editing. It simply involves taking one section of footage and placing it upon some kind of timeline. With any package there will be a variety of methods; this tutorial will show you just one. As you explore software, you will undoubtedly find newer and more efficient ways of handling these processes.

As a result of the importing process (see Appendix II) you will have a large number of smaller files that need to be trimmed and assembled to make the final film. For the purposes of this tutorial, the footage contained in each of these tutorials will be referred to as a 'clip'. This suggested editing method[7] is based around a single file, which forms the core of your film, onto which other files are added. This core clip should be the first chronological clip of the film:

1. Select any of the .avi files you have imported to be your core.
2. Open this file in VirtualDubMod (File>Open video file)
3. Next you will be adding a new clip of film to the core. The clip you select should be the clip that, according to your script or storyboard, will append your core clip.
4. Load in the next clip by selecting File>Append segment… This will open a window that allows you to select a new file. Select the clip that appends your core clip. This clip will then be added to the end of the existing film.
5. View this newly appended amalgamation of two clips by clicking on the Output Playback button.

Unless the new clip has been imported at precisely the correct length and the core clip is also cropped to exactly the correct length, the two clips will need 'tidying' to get them to match exactly.

6. To tidy this join up, play the footage until you reach the spot in your core clip where, according to your script or storyboard, the new appended clip should begin. To aid you in this process, you can move to any point in the footage by moving the mouse pointer onto the time line and clicking on it. You can also use the Forwards and Backwards buttons to fine-tune your location in the clip until you are at the exact frame required.

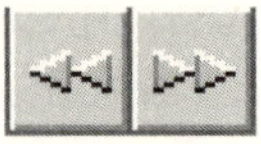

7. This is then marked. At the point you have selected click on the 'Mark in' button.

You will notice a small marker has appeared on the timeline to indicate this 'Mark in' point.

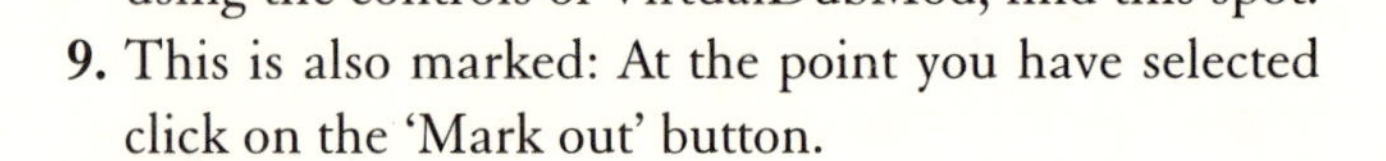

8. Now you need to mark the spot in your appended clip where the new clip should begin. Once more, using the controls of VirtualDubMod, find this spot.
9. This is also marked: At the point you have selected click on the 'Mark out' button.

You will notice another small marker has appeared on the timeline to indicate this 'Mark out' point. There will also be a darker bar of colour to shot the length of time that has been marked between the 'Mark in' and 'Mark out' points.

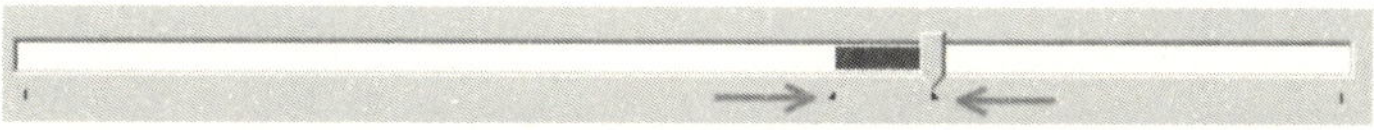

10. Finally, the footage that is not needed and that has been marked between the Mark in and Mark out points can now be deleted. To do this select Edit>Cut.

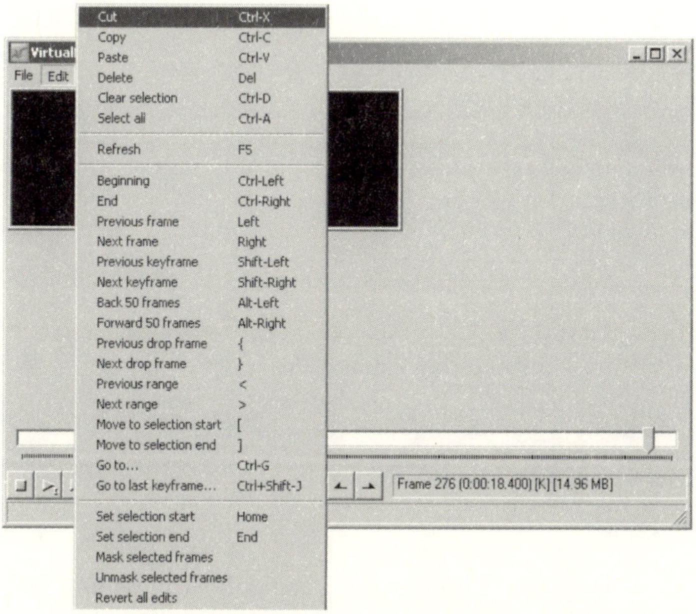

11. Then save your work. You will notice that each time you save, you must do so with a different filename – as VirtualDubMod only offers the 'Save As' option and you cannot save over the file you are working on. Save it (File>Save As) with the new name 'core.avi' – leave the settings for saving at default, so that all your work is being saved uncompressed.

This process is then repeated with the next clip in the film, and so on until the film has been assembled.

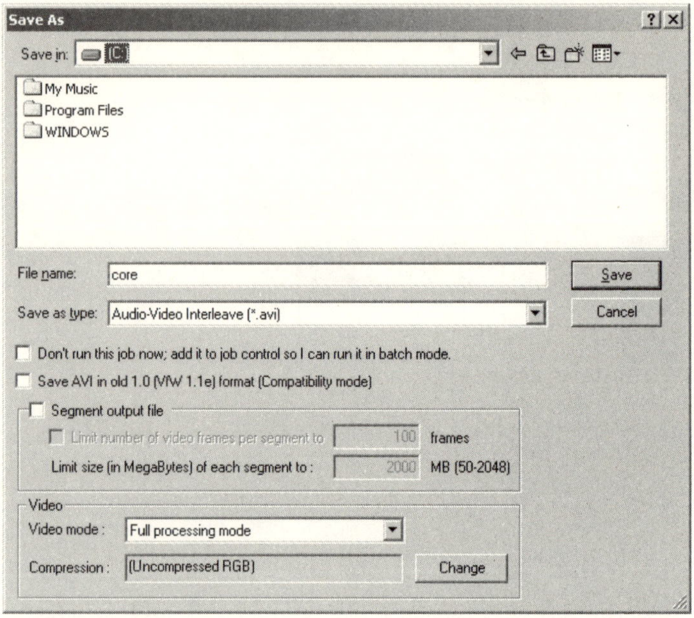

Edit Plus!

There is more that can be done using this editing tool. For example new clips can be added anywhere in the timeline by appending the clip you wish to add as described above, but placing the'Mark in' and 'Mark out' points around the clip you wish to keep, cutting it as described – then moving to the point on the timeline you wish to add the clip and selecting Edit>Paste and finally removing the unwanted appended footage by placing the 'Mark in' and 'Mark out' points around that you wish to delete and selecting Edit>Cut.

Adding Titles and Credits

Adding titles in VirtualDubMod is a slightly more complex matter than with other editing packages such as Premiere or

Final Cut Pro. It is done by taking an .avi file and overwriting it with a title screen.

1. Select any .avi file that you have imported which is long enough to be your tile or credit sequence.
2. Open this file in VirtualDubMod (File>Open video file).
3. The .tga's image will be added as a filter: Video> Filters… This will open the filters dialogue box.

4. From here click on the Add button and scroll down the list offered and select 'logo'.

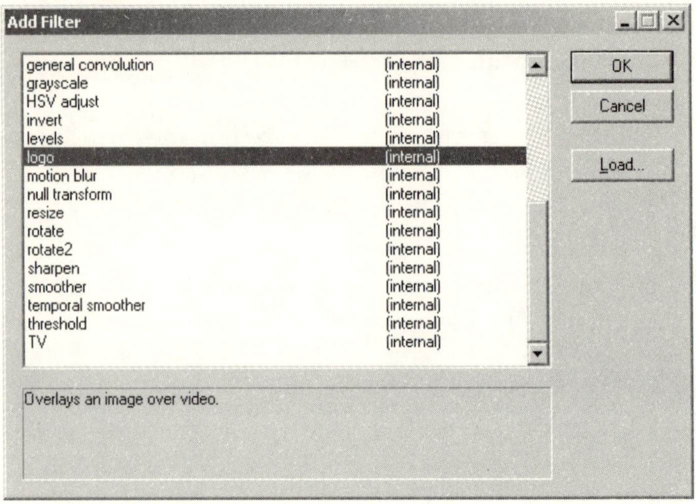

5. Then select the .tga to add (you can only do one at a time using this method) using the load button.

Leave the other settings as default and click OK.

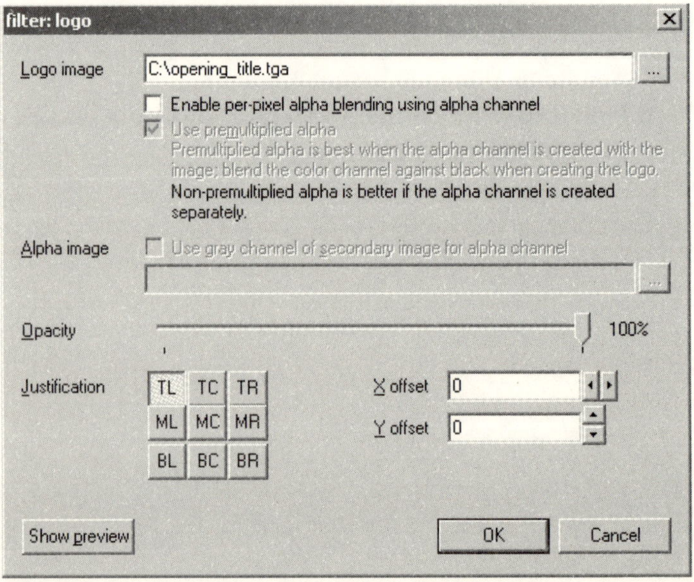

6. If you wish to remove the sound, you can do so by selecting Streams>Stream list and clicking on to the disable button.

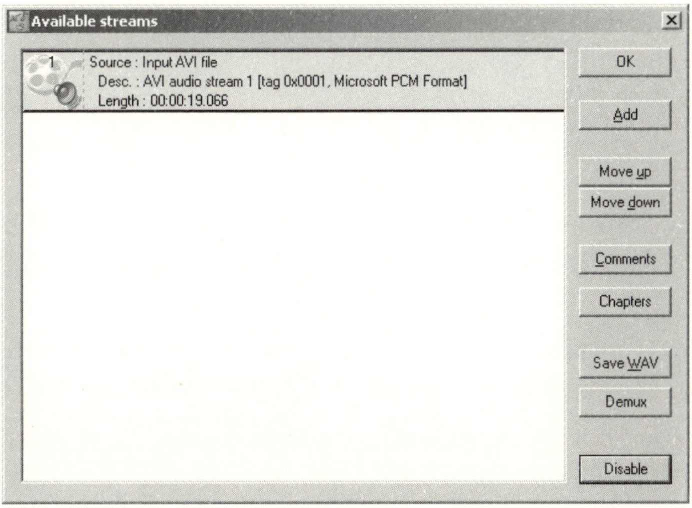

7. Save it (File>Save As) with the new name 'titles.avi'– this will ensure you do not overwrite the original clip with the titles. Leave the settings for saving at default, so that all your work is being saved uncompressed. This new file can then be added to your film using the methods described above.

Conclusion

Once you have produced a film you will then need to compress it for it to be of use as a web film. There is more information on this in Appendices IV and V. There are, in addition, other sources of support for VirtualDubMod including the main forums for VirtualDub and VirtualDubMod at http://virtualdub.everwicked.com and other forms of support such as on the VirtualDub site at http://www.virtualdub.org and Doom9.org, which has many guides such as how to add sound to a file (good for adding sound tracks[8]). Happy VirtualDubbing!

Although VirtualDubMod is a very basic editing package, with few of the features many people expect from non-linear editing packages, it does contain the basic tools needed to make a short film...it's also free!

References and Notes

1 The homepage of VirtualDub can be found at http://www.virtualdub.org. You may also wish to experiment with VirtualDub, as you may find it easier to work with and also that it has options that the modified version, Virtual DubMod, does not.

2 To donate see http://sourceforge.net/donate/index.php?group_id=65889

3 Information on QuickTime Pro can be found at http://www.apple.com/quicktime/upgrade

4 .tga, or Truevision Targa is the name given to a format developed by Truevision Inc (now called Pinnacle Systems) to store the position and colour details of each pixel in an image. See http://www.faqs.org/faqs/graphics/fileformats faq/part3/section146-.html. Many commonly found art packages such as Paint Shop Pro and Photoshop will create files in this format. VirtualDubMod does allow other file formats to be used, but .tga is by far the simplest to work with in this case.

5 This version, VirtualDubMod 1.5.10.1, came from the VirtualDubMod download page. http://sourceforge.net/project/showfiles.php?group_id=65889

6 At the time of writing, basic versions of both of these tools can be downloaded free. For Ultimate Zip see http://www.ultimatezip.com/index.php and for WinRAR see http://www.rarlab.com

7 This is only a suggested method. Due to the non-linear nature of digital editing it is possible to edit in any number of different ways.

8 For the guide to adding sound to an .avi file see http://www.doom9.org/index.html?/virtualdub_procedures.htm and select the option 'Joining uncompressed audio and compressed video (including MP3 audio compression).'

Appendix IV: Distributing Films on a File Trade Network

Free Filmmaking

In this section we are aiming to give a glimpse of the filmmaking process whilst adhering to the standards outlined by the Free Software Foundation (see Chapter 3). As such, we are intending to use free versions of the following software: editing tools, codec and distribution systems. If you have no interest in the Free Software aspect of this appendix and are looking for information on distributing using a file trade network then skip the next two sections and start on the section on using Gnutella. It is possible to use other editing software to achieve the same result as file trade networks can be used to distribute any format of file you wish.

Getting Started

In the following section we will take you through the process of making your films easily accessible to most internet users and then making them freely available on a file trade network. To begin this you will need the following:

- A computer with an internet connection.
- An edited version of your film in the .avi file format
- A client (like a web browser used on file trade networks) that allows you to connect to the Gnutella network.
- The OpenDivX Code (as above).
- Software to apply this codec to your films.

Most editing software will allow you to export your films as an .avi. When you export the films simply look at the 'Save as' options (see Appendix III) and select the appropriate file format. If your software does not allow you to export in this format, try another one such as MPEG-4. You will be able to export your film as many times as you wish – so don't be afraid to experiment.

The Gnutella network is a peer-to-peer or file trading network. There are other networks, but this is the one we have chosen as our example. The Gnutella network requires you to use a 'client' to connect to the network – this is simply software that can browse this network, in a similar way that a web browser allows you to view websites. The one that plugincinema uses is called Gnucleus, but there is a list of various clients for various operating systems on the Gnutella website – http://www.gnutella.com/connect – you will find most of these software clients are available either free of charge or request a small donation. (IMPORTANT: before using the network, take time to ensure the security of your computer. See Chapter 11 for more information on this.)

The codec we will be using is a piece of software that compresses and decompresses movie files, so making them into a manageable size. For this example we are suggesting the use of the OpenDivX Codec by Project Mayo. There are plenty of other codecs, but we are recommending this one as it is widely used, easily viewable by many media players and free (cost-wise) and free (free as in copyright freedom)[1]. This codec can be downloaded free from http://www.projectmayo.com/projects – scroll down then select and download the OpenDivX for your operating system. We are using the Windows version – so select 'OpenDivX for Windows' and select the 'OpenDivX Install File (*.exe)' option. (If this codec is not available for your operating system, then try one that is: such as MPEG-4. However, if your films are already MPEG-4 and you cannot find an OpenDivX codec for your operating system, then skip this step and go straight to the installation on the Gnutella client.)

To compress your films using the OpenDivX codec, you

will need some software that can apply it. We are suggesting you use VirtualDubMod, which can be found at http://virtualdubmod.sourceforge.net. We have chosen this particular software because the open version of DivX is not supported by Adobe Premiere. The use of VirtualDubMod continues our intention of using Free Software where possible.

Creating OpenDivX Films

Once you have all you need, you can begin the process of encoding your .avi film so that it works using OpenDivX:

1. Install the OpenDivX codec. As we had downloaded the 'OpenDivX Install File (*.exe)' option, this is a simple matter of locating this file and running it. It will install without any fuss, into the area of the operating system that stores codecs.
2. Locate and unzip the version of VirtualDubMod you have downloaded. This guide has been created using VirtualDubMod version 1.5.10.1. When downloaded from the internet it was compressed as a .zip file (see Chapter 10 for more on this) and to unzip it you will need a piece of software such as Ultimate Zip or WinRAR.[2] If you have such a tool installed you will be able to click on the file and unzip it. On a windows machine this can be done by right-clicking on the file and selecting 'Extract to Folder' etc.
3. Run VirtualDubMod. In Windows, this is done by running the file 'VirtualDubMod.exe'.
4. Using VirtualDubMod, open your .avi file.

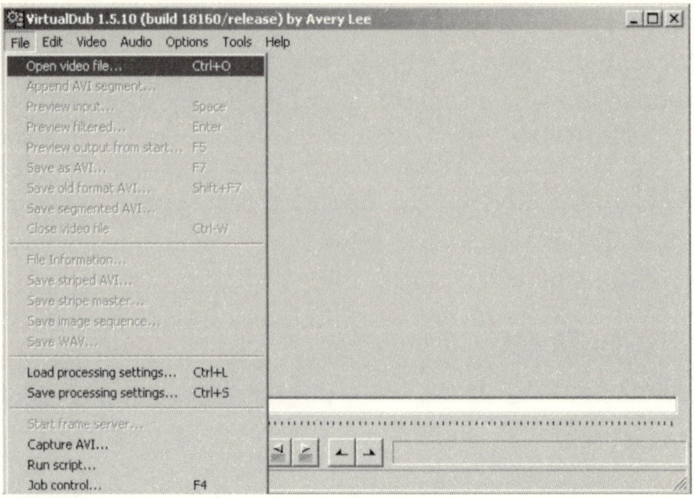

5. Select 'Video>Compression'. This will open the compression dialogue box. From the list offered select the 'DivX MPEG-4 Codec (4.0 a50)'. This is the OpenDivX codec. Then click 'OK'. (Note this name might change slightly if you have installed a different version of the OpenDivX codec.)

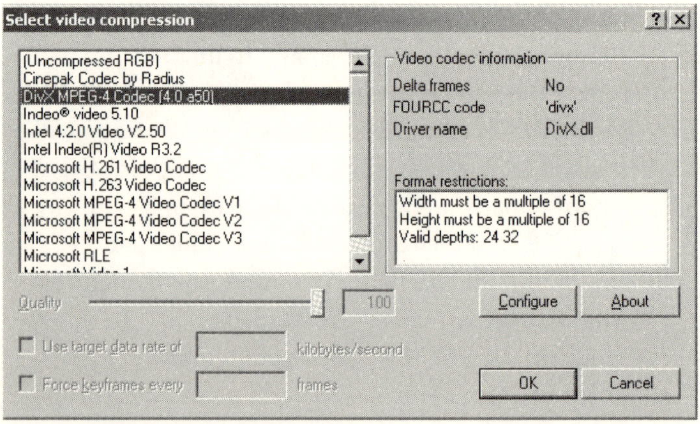

6. Then select 'File>Save', ensure it will save it as an .avi, give it a new name and save it. This saving process will take time, depending on the size of your original file,

as VirtualDubMod has to re-compress the film.

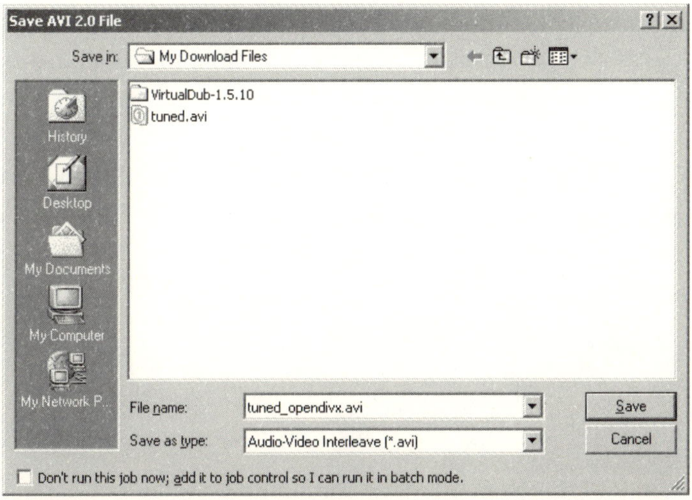

7. Now select 'Streams>Video Comment' – this will open a new box where you can enter file information such as the title and add it to the file – as discussed in Chapter 11.

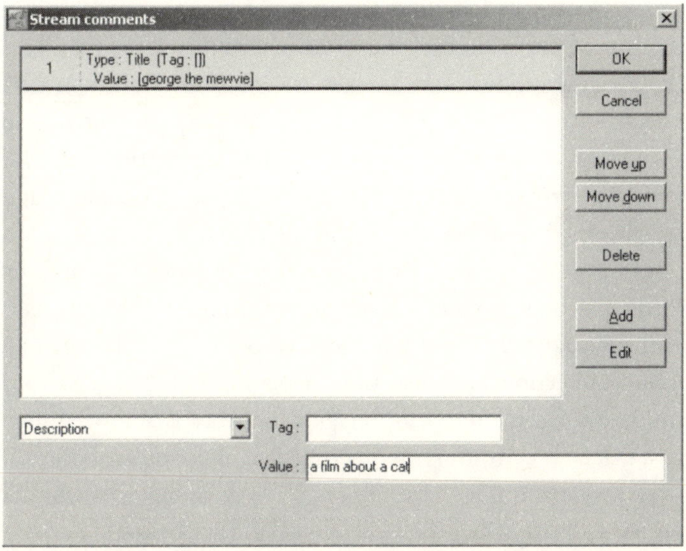

Using Gnutella

Once you have your film ready to distribute, you now need to install your Gnutella client. In the example used, this is Gnucleus. There are many options for clients on the Gnutella website, listed by operating system. Any client selected should still operate in a similar manner to Gnucleus.

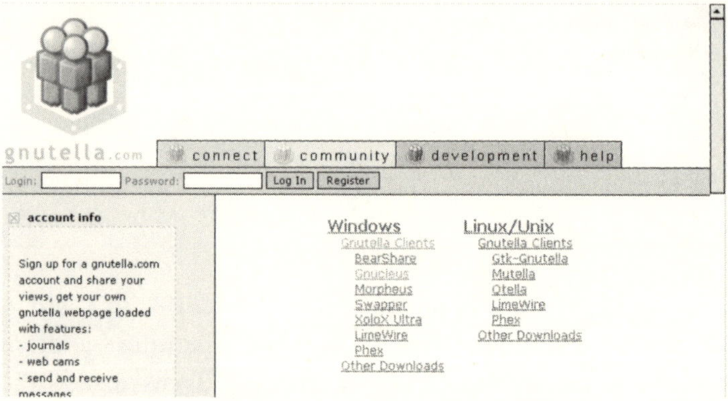

A shot of the Gnutella webpage with a list of possible clients.

Once this is installed, place the film you wish to distribute into the shared folder. In the case of Gnucleus this default folder is 'C:\Program Files\Gnucleus\Downloads' though you can check this or change it by selecting 'Edit>Preferences' and selecting the 'Share' option on the left-hand bar. This will allow you to access a screen from which you can change, add or remove shared directories. (See below.)

Once your film is in this directory you need to run the Gnutella client, if you have not already done so. The program will automatically attempt to connect to the Gnutella network. This connection may take time depending on how fast your internet connection is, how busy the network is and what time of day it is. It is worth remembering that as the bulk of peer-to-peer network traffic comes from the U.S., most networks are far more active when the U.S. is awake! (See below.)

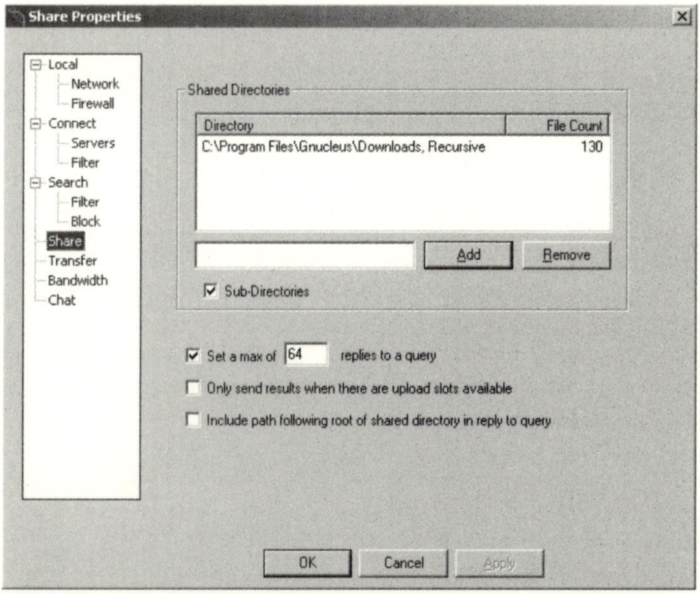

The Gnucleus screen indicating it is connecting to the Gnutella network.

Once the connection has been established, you are open for business. Whilst your computer is connected to this network, other users searching for your film can download it from your shared folder. The longer you are connected and the more time people have to search your machine, the more people will be able to download your film and the more your film will spread. Welcome to the file-trade revolution!

References and Notes

1 Richard Stallman, founder of the Free Software Foundation suggested this codec to us in an email: 'There is free software available for Divx, called Opendivx. There are patents covering Divx, and someday they may be used to wipe out Opendivx, but as long as it remains available as free software, I think it is ok to use. This format is more compressed than Mpeg1 so you might consider it advantageous to use.'

2 At the time of writing basic versions of both of these tools can be downloaded free. For Ultimate Zip see http://www.ultimatezip.com/index.php and for WinRAR see http://www.rarlab.com

Appendix V: Encoding Using QuickTime Pro 5

As it would not be practical to cover the multitude of obtainable methods and options for the huge number of compression technologies currently available, this chapter elects to examine just one method of encoding in detail – to give the reader a basic idea of the process involved. In this way, by examining a single compression process, we can give both a practical example of compression and an overview of the whole process. This example is performed on an uncompressed film using Apple's QuickTime Pro 5[1] on a machine running Windows XP.

1. First import the film of your choice (this can be a QuickTime movie, uncompressed AVI or MPEG depending on what formats the encoding software supports). Click on '**File**' on the top menu bar, then from the pop-up menu select '**Import**' (the notation we are using for this from here onwards is **File > Import**).

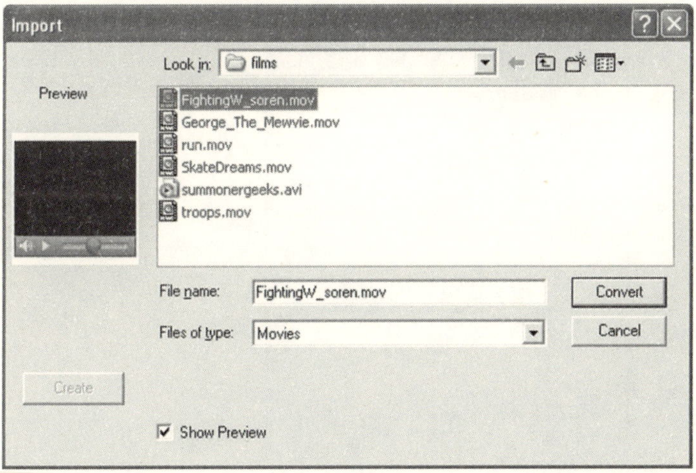

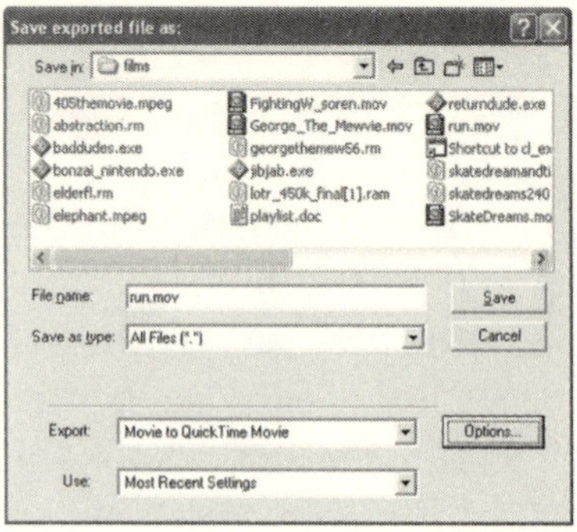

2. You will then need to export the film (to QuickTime, MPEG or AVI): click on File > Export. In the 'Save exported file as' window you will be able to select which format to encode your film to by clicking on the 'Export' drop-down box. In this example we have elected for QuickTime. You will also be faced with the option to either use one of QuickTime's pre-set setting or to customise the setting yourself. To use one of the pre-sets click on the 'Use' drop-down box to select the desired streaming settings and then click on 'Save'.

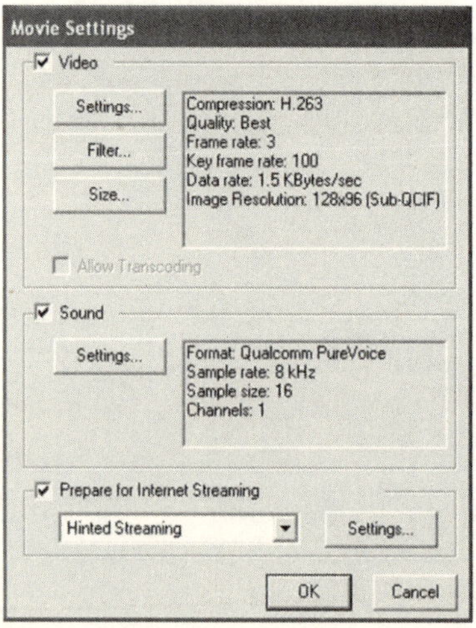

3. Alternatively, if you want to customise the setting click on 'Options'. In 'Movie Settings' make sure both the 'Video' and 'Sound' checkboxes are ticked. Here you will see a summary of the encoding settings, all of which can be modified. To change the video settings click on the 'Settings' button in the 'Video' box. (See above.)
4. In the 'Compression Settings' window you can select the compressor of your choice from the drop-down box. Apple recommend using Sorenson Video 3, H.261, H.263, or Motion JPEG for video, but what you see will largely depend on the compressors you have available on your computer. You can vary the image quality: choosing 'Best' will give a clearer image but in return will make the final file size larger.

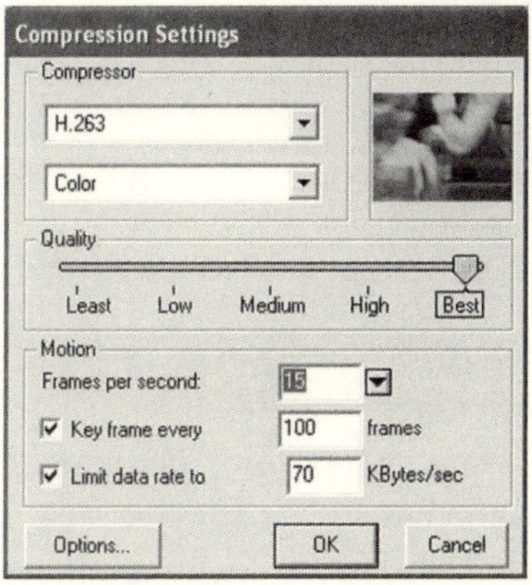

5. In the 'Motion' box you can select the frames per second: fifteen is usually a safe bet, but use more if you want smoother motion and less if the motion is not top priority.
6. Setting key frames can be a fine art depending on the bandwidth limits of the intended film viewer. For those of you who have never had the pleasure of encountering key frames their purpose is fairly simple: they

contain all of the necessary bits of movie information, while subsequent frames contain only the information that has changed. If you have too many key frames, you will get a larger movie with a higher data rate, however, too few result in a low quality movie.

7. The data rate is the amount of data that is played every second and only a few of the compressors allow you to customize this. It is important that it is set at an appropriate level for its intended bandwidth: low for dial-up modem users (6-10 KBytes/sec) and higher for broadband. Click on 'OK' to take you back to the 'Movie Settings' window, or 'Options' to take you to the compressor's 'Encoder Options', where you can set the resolution of the encoded film.

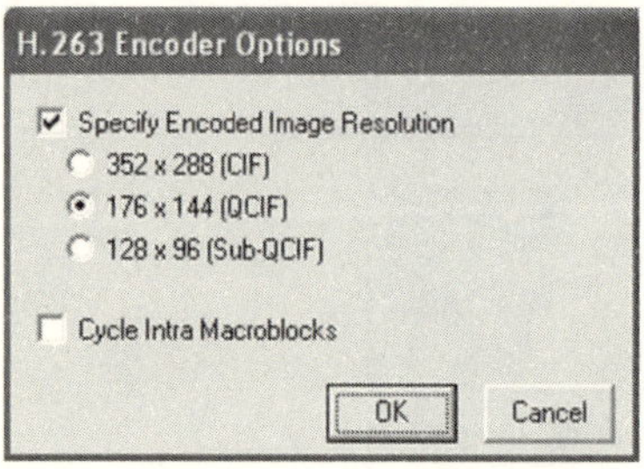

8. Back in the 'Movie Settings' window click on 'Size' in the 'Video' box to get the 'Export Size' Settings. (See below). Here you can chose to use the film's current size, or you can change the size to anything you wish. Remember that the smaller the dimensions of the film, the smaller the end file size. Click on 'OK' to take you back to the 'Movie Settings' window.
9. To change the audio settings click on 'Settings' in the 'Audio' box back in the 'Movie Settings' window. In the 'Sound Settings' window you can choose which audio compressor to use from the drop-down box. Apple recommends DVI 4:1, QDesign Music 2, QUALCOMM PureVoice and uLaw 2:1 for audio,

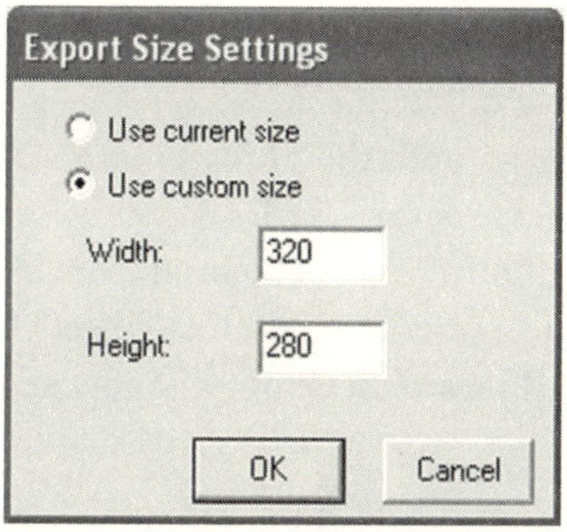

but your choice will largely depend on the particular audio content of your film: whether it is purely music or voice, or a combination of the two. You can also set the data rate of the audio. Remember that 44.1 kHz, 16 bit Stereo is equivalent in quality to a compact disc, so anything less will give lower quality audio and in turn reduce the end file size of your clip. If the sound is not that important take the data rate right down and select 'Mono', if the option is available.

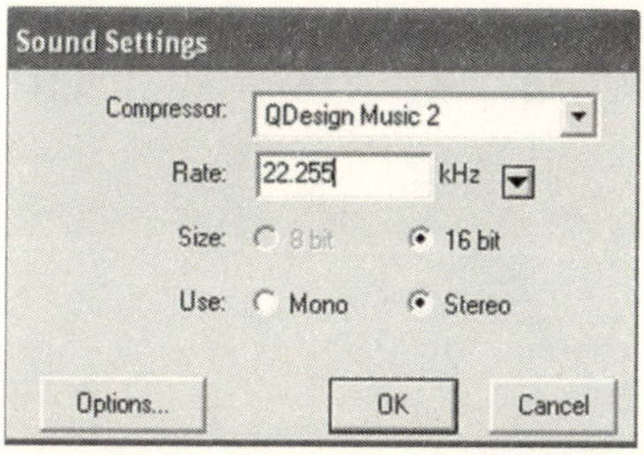

10. Once you are happy with these settings, click 'OK', to take you back to the 'Save exported file as' window and click on 'Save'. The length of time taken to encode the film will depend largely on the size of the original film and the speed of your computer. In most cases you will have to encode several versions of your film to find the one that gives the best results. If your original film is quite long, it may be worth

considering taking just a small clip of it, and encoding that, using different settings.

11. Finally, you need to add the 'Movie Info' (also referred to as meta data). Re-load your newly encoded film into QuickTime. Click on 'Movie' to open the drop-down menu, and then select 'Get Movie Properties'. The screen below will appear.

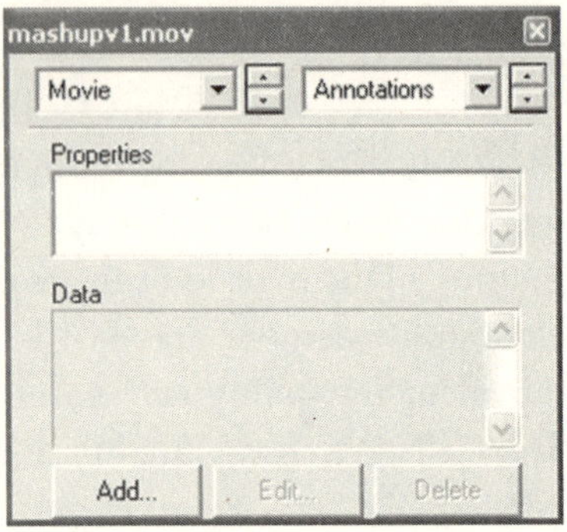

Click on 'Add…'. From here you may select the types of annotation (e.g. director, copyright, artist) you wish to add and fill in the relevant information in the box below. When saved, this data will be incorporated into the file.

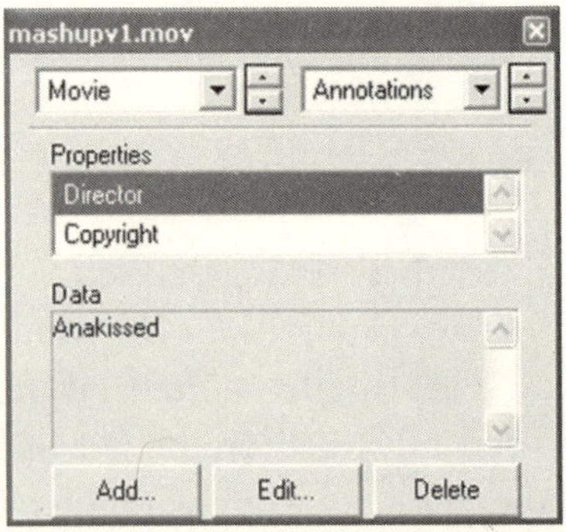

Although this example uses QuickTime Pro 5, most encoding software will provide similar options to those discussed above.

Conclusion

In summary, compression technologies are currently an integral part of the production process when making films for the internet and it will be a far smoother process if you work with these tools rather than against them. Each separate piece of compression software or hardware will have its own unique affect upon the work you have produced. Experimenting with both the settings and types of compression that can be applied can be a painstaking process, but for the web filmmaker it is both vital and rewarding.

You can find out more about the Apple program QuickTimePro at the website for this software at http://www.apple.com/quicktime. Plus Apple have a Help & Support site at http://www.info.apple.com.

Links for Further Doing

Apple's QuickTime Site
http://www.apple.com/quicktime

Apple's Help & Support Site
http://www.info.apple.com

MPEG Homepage
http://www.chiariglione.org/mpeg

New Media Republic website, 'What is Compression?'
http://newmediarepublic.com/dvideo/compression/adv04.html

plugincinema's forum to discuss your ideas and practices
http://www.plugincinema.com/plugin/forum

References and Notes

1 For more on QuickTime Pro see **http://www.apple.com/quicktime/upgrade**

Appendix VI: Creating a Webpage for Free

Why Use HTML?

This tutorial will focus on creating a webpage for free, that is, without any software being needed and using HTML – the language that websites are created in. This might look technical, but it is recommended that you try it for several reasons:

- It is a good way to overcome any techno-fear. You will be grappling with something new but achievable and at the same time familiarizing yourself with a technical environment.
- It gives you a good idea of what is going on 'under the bonnet' of a website.
- What you learn here provides a useful grounding for future projects where you might use web design software or work with other people.
- Websites are a useful promotional tool for marketing your film and if you feel at all confident with the technology involved, it would be advisable to set one up personally. Otherwise, if you don't understand any HTML and something goes wrong with your site, it will be much harder to fix it yourself.

This tutorial is going to explain how to create a website with the following basic features which, as a web filmmaker, you may find useful on your site:

- A link to your film.
- Contact details.
- Images.

Note that you can get the sample image and film used in creating this site from the plugincinema.com website at http://www. plugincinema.com/plugin/book.htm.

Introducing HTML

A website normally consists of a number of components. Central to the viewing experience are the webpages themselves, and these will be written in HTML which is a scripting language and is one of the building blocks of the internet. We suggest writing your webpage using a text editor (this is a simplified version of a word processor); if you are using windows you could use Notepad and if you are using an Apple Mac you could use Simple Text.[1] Alternatively you can download a free HTML editor, which can be useful as they offer additional functionality, but if you are new to this we suggest keeping it simple and using one of the packages already discussed in Chapter 11.

Building the Basic Skeleton

Run the text editor, this will present you with a blank new page. First you need to type in the basic structure of an HTML page. This consists of three sets of 'tags'. These tags exist in pairs and each are enclosed in '<' and '>' symbols, with the final tag beginning with '/'. So, type the following:

```
<HTML>
<HEAD>
</HEAD>
<BODY>
</BODY>
</HTML>
```

This has created a page with three important structures; the HTML component establishes that the script within the tags is written in the HTML language. The HEAD tags establish a place to store the entire header (or preparatory information about the webpage) and the BODY tags establish a place to store the actual content of the webpage.

Now you need to save your work and in Notepad this is done by selecting 'File>Save'. You will be presented with a box to enter the file name. Call this page 'index.html' and click OK. (When a web browser, such as Internet Explorer, looks into a directory containing webpages it looks for a file called index or home first.) It is important that you add the '.html' at the end of the name so that your computer recognizes that this is an HTML file and not just a text file.

Now load this webpage to test that it works. This can be done by opening your web browser – this example is shown using Internet Explorer. Select 'File>Open' which will cause a dialogue box to appear.

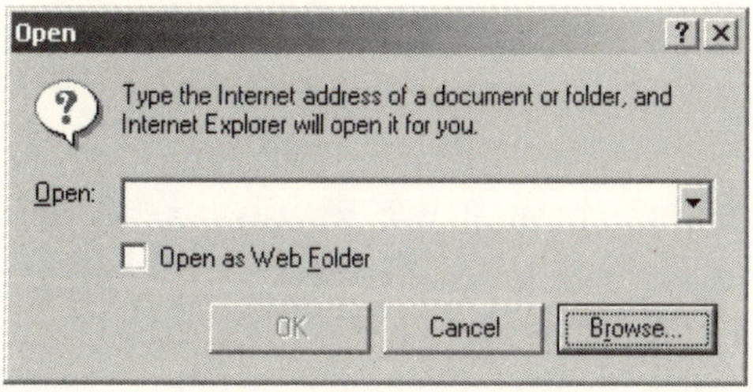

From this select the 'Browse' button and select the 'index.html' file you have created and click 'OK'. A blank webpage should appear. You will find it easier if you leave both the Notepad file and the web browser open while you work.

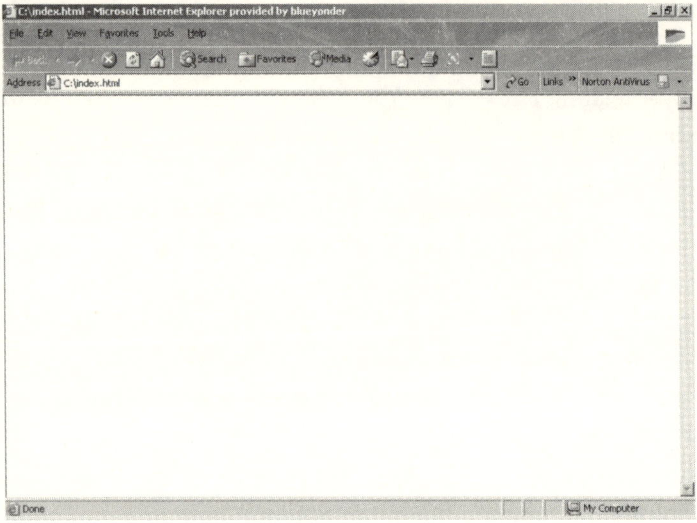

Putting Flesh on the Bones

Now you have created the basic structure, it is time to start adding some content. Return to the Notepad page and add the following text to what has already been written. (Note that although new text is displayed in bold type here to make it easier for you to see what has been added, you do not need to use any bold type in your text file):

<HTML>
<HEAD>
<TITLE>George the Mewvie!</TITLE>
</HEAD>
<BODY>
George the Mewvie – a film about a cat!
</BODY>
</HTML>

Once you have typed this, save your work. Then return to your web browser and click the refresh button (on Internet Explorer the button looks like a recycle symbol). This will re-load the webpage you are working on. You will now notice two changes: the addition of a title in the title bar of the web browser and some text in the window. (If you are having trouble seeing any of this possible problems could be that you have saved your work as a text file and not an .html file, or that the page has not reloaded. To check the latter try forcing the web browser to reload the page as if it were a new page. Using Internet Explorer this is done by holding down the Control (Ctrl) key and clicking on the refresh button.)

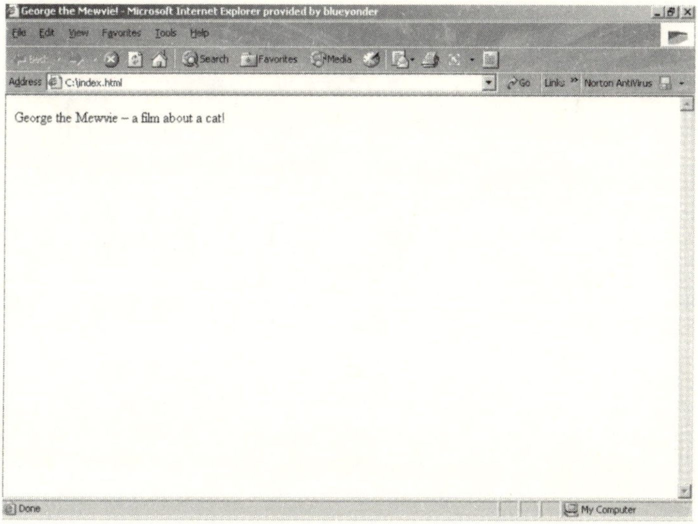

Now we need to add more text to provide further information about the film. As more text is added, more tags also need to be added to control the way the text looks. There are a variety of ways to do this, but this tutorial will focus on using the following tags to control the text:

- Displaying text in a large format – **<H1>** and **</H1>**
- Displaying text in a normal sized format – **<H4>** and **</H4>**

- Displaying text in a small sized format – **<H5>** and **</H5>**
- Ending a paragraph – **<P>** (You will notice that this tag is not being used as part of a pair).

```
<HTML>
<HEAD>
<TITLE>George the Mewvie!</TITLE>
</HEAD>
<BODY>
<H1>George the Mewvie – a film about a
cat!</H1><P>
<H4>George the Mewvie is a film about a cat. Not
just any cat, but a special cat. The film is intended to
capture the look and feel of a cats fur by allowing the
compression to run riot over the footage that has been
shot.</H4><P>
<H5>Contact information: ana@pluginmanifesto.com
</H5>
</BODY>
</HTML>
```

Once more, after you have finished typing this, save your work. Then return to your web browser and click the refresh button again. Your webpage should now look something like this:

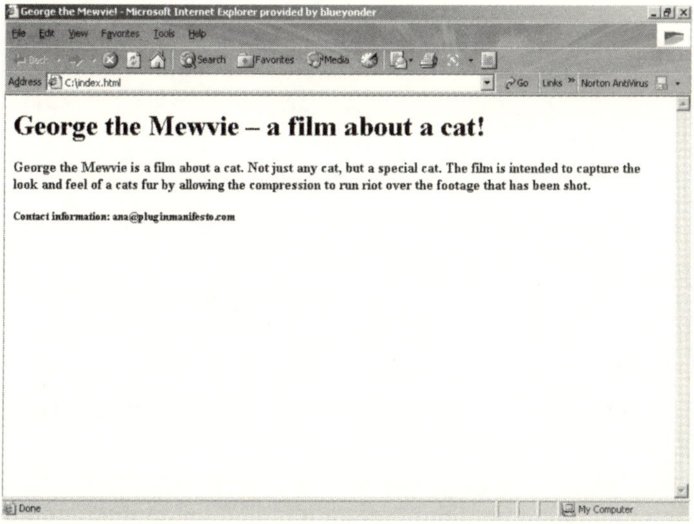

Colour Me Bad

Now we can add some colour to the website. There are a large number of methods you can use to alter colours or to provide certain styles throughout, but we will focus on simply changing the colour of the text and the background. As HTML is all text, colour information is stored as a code; in this case a hexadecimal code (this is a base 16 numbering convention rather than the base 10 we most often encounter – but do not worry – as you do not need to be able to count in hex!). This hexadecimal code is placed, alongside a little HTML, inside the <BODY> tag that has already been written. The HTML added here is BGCOLOR to represent the background colour (note HTML uses the US spelling) and TEXT to represent the text colour. The colour codes chosen in this example are #000000 which is black and #ffffff which is white. You can find a useful list of hexadecimal colour codes at http://www.december.com/html/spec/color.html and a website that allows you to experiment with colours at http://catless.ncl.ac.uk/php/misc/colours.php.

```
<HTML>
<HEAD>
<TITLE>George the Mewvie!</TITLE>
</HEAD>
<BODY BGCOLOR=#000000 TEXT=#ffffff>
<H1>George the Mewvie – a film about a cat!</H1><P>
<H4>George the Mewvie is a film about a cat. Not just any cat, but a special cat. The film is intended to capture the look and feel of a cat's fur by allowing the compression to run riot over the footage that has been shot.</H4><P>
<H5>Contact information:
ana@pluginmanifesto.com</H5>
</BODY>
</HTML>
```

Once more, when this has been typed, save your work. Then return to your web browser and click the refresh button. Your webpage should now appear in a different colour (in this black and white image only the shade and tone will look different).

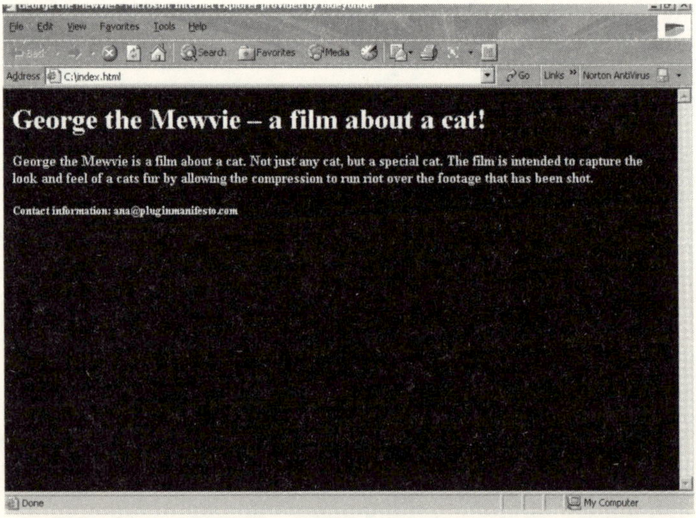

The colour tags you have added change the colour of all the text within the pair of the <BODY> and </BODY> tags. You can change the colour of text within this section further by using separate FONT tags. In this case, adding a pair of FONT tags around some words to give then a different colour, to give dark grey for example, which is represented by the colour code #828282.

```
<HTML>
<HEAD>
<TITLE>George the Mewvie!</TITLE>
</HEAD>
<BODY BGCOLOR=#000000 TEXT=#ffffff>
<H1>George the Mewvie – <FONT COLOR=
#828282> a film about a cat!</FONT>
</H1><P>
<H4>George the Mewvie is a film about a cat. Not
just any cat, but a special cat. The film is intended to
capture the look and feel of a cat's fur by allowing the
compression to run riot over the footage that has been
shot.</H4><P>
<H5>Contact information:
ana@pluginmanifesto.com</H5>
</BODY>
</HTML>
```

Once more, when this has been typed, save your work. Then return to your web browser and click the refresh button. The latter part of the title should now appear in a different colour (though in these black and white reproductions it will simply look a shade darker).

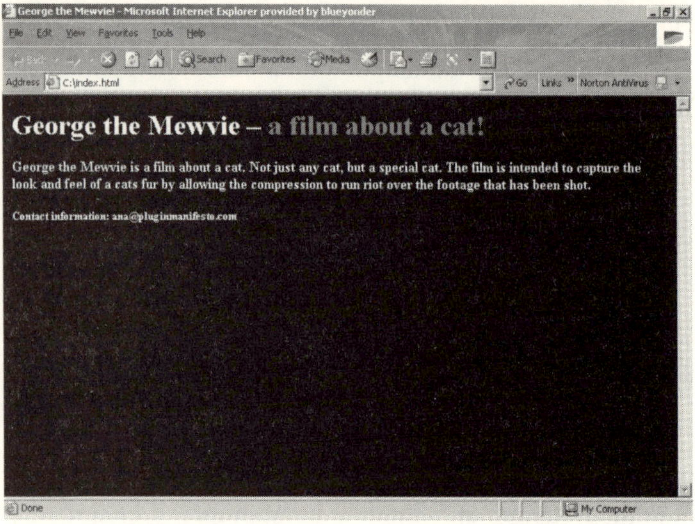

Image Conscious

Next we will add an image to the website. As HTML is only text, adding an image is done by loading an image into the webpage. The most common image format used on the internet is the .jpeg (or .jpg) and .gif file types. (For more on these see Chapter 10.) Most graphics and image software will allow you to save images in these formats.[2] This example uses an image with the file name 'george_film.jpg'. This file name is encased in an image tag <IMG SRC= "path and name" alt= "image info"> where the path and name includes the full path for the webpage on the server where the site is stored, for example, if the image was stored in a directory called 'pictures' this would be 'pictures/george_film.jpg'. In contrast, image information can include any text information you wish about the image – note that you do not have to provide this information, but it is a good idea! Added into the page the HTML looks like:

```
<HTML>
<HEAD>
<TITLE>George the Mewvie!</TITLE>
```

```
</HEAD>
<BODY BGCOLOR=#000000 TEXT=#ffffff>
<H1>George the Mewvie – <FONT COLOR=#
828282> a film about a cat!</FONT></H1><P>
<H4>George the Mewvie is a film about a cat. Not
just any cat, but a special cat. The film is intended to
capture the look and feel of a cat’s fur by allowing the
compression to run riot over the footage that has been
shot.</H4><P>
<H5>Contact information:
ana@pluginmanifesto.com</H5>
<P>
<IMG SRC=“george_film.jpg”alt=“A still from
George the Mewvie”>
<P>
</BODY>
</HTML>
```

When this has been typed, save your work, return to your web browser and click the refresh button. Your webpage should now look something like this:

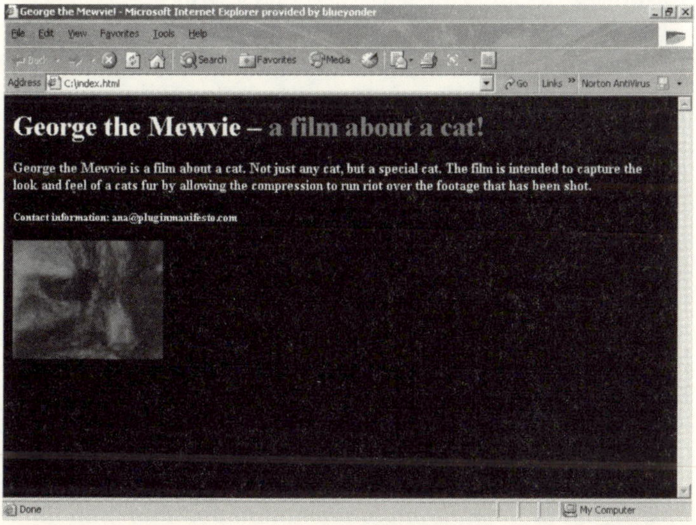

Organize & Communicate!

Now we will add some links into the website. Links, or to give them their correct name, 'Hyperlinks', are the means by which the internet becomes so powerful. This ability to link a webpage to any other webpage, on any other site, is what gives the internet its unique interconnected nature. Let us assume that you have followed two of the other tutorials and made an OpenDivX version of your film for use with the Gnutella network (Appendix IV) and you have also encoded a QuickTime version of your film (Appendix V) to be streamed from your website. As a result you will have a QuickTime file, in this example it is called 'george.mov'.

Before the links can be added, we need to type in the appropriate information about these links. It is also advisable to investigate various tools which will enhance the flow and layout of the information in your website. In this example we will be using some table tags. Table tags are always enclosed inside a pair of <TABLE> and </TABLE> tags. Within these are tags to create individual cells – <TD> and </TD> – and rows – <TR> and </TR>. To make a table with two rows and two cells, the HTML will be:

```
<HTML>
<HEAD>
<TITLE>George the Mewvie!</TITLE>
</HEAD>
<BODY BGCOLOR=#000000 TEXT=#ffffff>
<H1>George the Mewvie – <FONT COLOR=#828282> a film about a cat!</FONT></H1><P>
<H4>George the Mewvie is a film about a cat. Not just any cat, but a special cat. The film is intended to capture the look and feel of a cat's fur by allowing the compression to run riot over the footage that has been shot.</H4><P>
```

```
<H5>Contact information:
ana@pluginmanifesto.com</H5>
<P>
<IMG SRC="george_film.jpg"alt="A still from
George the Mewvie">
<P>
You can watch George the Mewvie:
<P>
<TABLE BORDER=ON>
<TR>
<TD>
If you wish to see the OpenDivX version, you can do
so by logging onto to Gnutella network. Start a search
for 'george' – you will get the best results if you do this
on the weekend, when I am also connected to the
network!
</TD>
<TD>
Gnutella
</TD>

<TR>
<TD>
If you wish to see the QuickTime version, you can do
so by streaming it from this site:
</TD>
<TD>
QuickTime
</TD>

</TR>
</TABLE>
</BODY>
</HTML>
```

Once more, when this has been typed, save your work. Then

return to your web browser and click the refresh button. Your webpage should now look something like this:

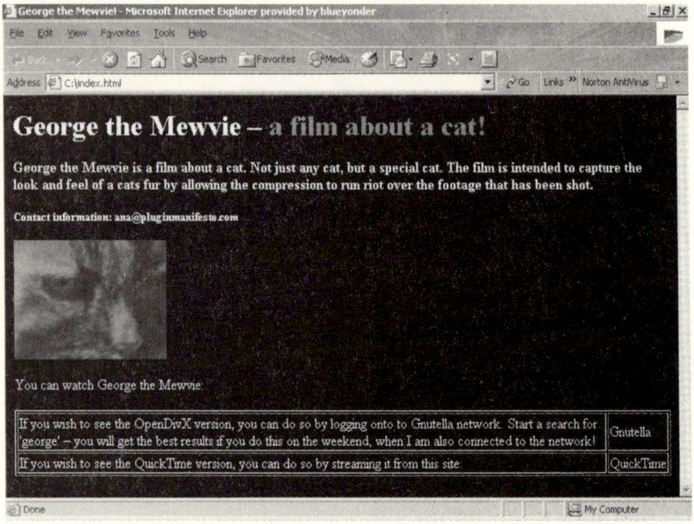

Now we need to add in the links. This is done by placing <A HREF> and </A> tags around the text or image that you wish to be the link. Inside the <A HREF> tag will then be placed the information about where the link is going. In this case one link will go to the website Gnutella.com and the other link will go to the QuickTime film called 'george.mov'.

Note: You do not need another website to technically do anything for you to be able to link to them, and it is common practice on the internet to simply link to whomever you wish. When you link to another website you need to ensure you have the full path including http:// and so on. In this example the full path is 'http://www.gnutella.com'.

To add two links, the HTML will be:

```
<HTML>
```

```
<HEAD>
<TITLE>George the Mewvie!</TITLE>
</HEAD>
<BODY BGCOLOR=#000000 TEXT=#ffffff>
<H1>George the Mewvie – <FONT COLOR=#828282> a film about a cat!</FONT></H1><P>
<H4>George the Mewvie is a film about a cat. Not just any cat, but a special cat. The film is intended to capture the look and feel of a cats fur by allowing the compression to run riot over the footage that has been shot.</H4><P>
<H5>Contact information:
ana@pluginmanifesto.com</H5>
<P>
<IMG SRC="george_film.jpg" alt= "A still from George the Mewvie">
<P>
You can watch George the Mewvie:
<P>
<TABLE BORDER=ON>
<TR>
<TD>
If you wish to see the OpenDivX version, you can do so by logging onto to the Gnutella network. Start a search for 'george' – you will get the best results if you do this on the weekend, when I am also connected to the network!
</TD>
<TD>
<A
HREF=http://www.gnutella.com>Gnutella</A>
</TD>

<TR>
<TD>
```

```
If you wish to see the QuickTime version, you can do so
by streaming it from this site:
</TD>
<TD>
<A HREF= "george.mov">QuickTime</A>
</TD>

</TR>
</TABLE>
</BODY>
</HTML>
```

Once more, when this has been typed, save your work. Then return to your web browser and click the refresh button. You should notice that the words 'Gnutella' and 'QuickTime' are underlined and can now be clicked on:

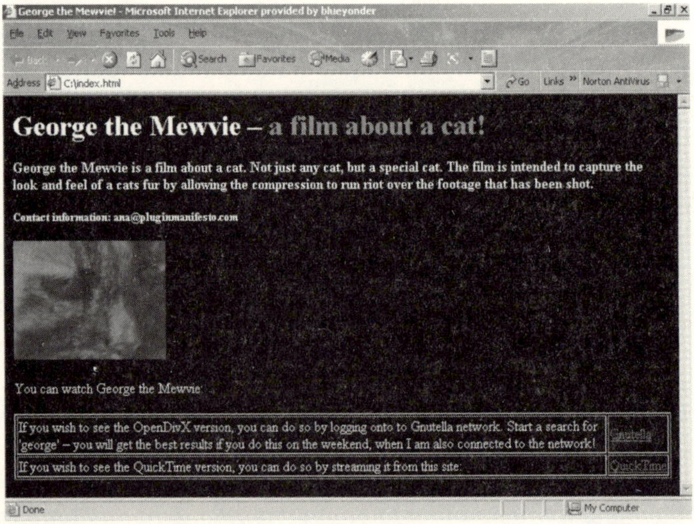

HTML Up your Life

You have now created a basic webpage! From here you would need to find a server to host the website you have just created so that it is accessible on the internet (see Chapter 11). This tutorial is a very brief introduction to websites and HTML. There is so much you can do, for example, the colours of the hyperlinked words can be changed, tables can be aligned to the left or right, different fonts can be used for text and so on. There are many more additions to the tags you have encountered and new tags to discover! There are a number of good resources that will take you further down this path. 'The Bare Bones Guide to HTML' at http://werbach.com/barebones/barebones.html and 'HTML: An Interactive Tutorial for Beginners' (aka Dave's HTML Guide) at http://www.davesite.com/webstation/html are good places to start.

Good luck!

References and Notes

1 You can find a little more information on text editors here http://www.kaidan.com/autolycus/reference/specifics/texteditor.html

2 Example software packages you could use for this include JASC software's Paint Shop Pro at http://www.jasc.com or try one of the packages listed on the Free Software Foundations website at http://www.fsf.org/directory/graphics/editors or from cover discs that computer magazines distribute.

Appendix VII: Using PayPal to Accept Money over the Internet

Introduction

This tutorial will guide you though the process of using PayPal to sell something using the internet. This item could be your film, a subscription and so on. It does not cover the mechanics of setting up a shop or a membership system to manage subscribers.

Note: This tutorial is not a blanket endorsement of this system; it just shows the use of it. Readers should also be aware that there are scams that target the users of PayPal and other similar systems.[1]

Why PayPal?

PayPal is a system that allows the transfer of funds securely between two people over the internet. What makes this system useful is its ease of use and flexibility. The two people involved can be anything from employees of a large company to ordinary individuals. The terms of the transfer are easy to set and the system allows messages to be sent with the money. PayPal alone is not a full shopping system (by this we mean something like that found on system's like dSWAT.net where goods are listed, selected items are placed in a virtual basket and then paid for at the virtual till using a credit card), but rather a money transfer system.[2]

How Does PayPal Work?

For an exchange of funds to happen, both parties need a PayPal account. The person wishing to buy will simply click on the PayPal button (or a similar method) that the seller has on their website. This will take the buyer to a PayPal secure site where s/he inputs the amount they wish to spend, any message for the seller (such as what the money is for or special delivery instructions) and enters their PayPal password – and that's it! As PayPal has the address for both, it sends the relevant information and transfers the funds between the PayPal accounts. These accounts can also have money placed in them or taken out using a credit card or similar.

Adding PayPal to a Website

The PayPal payment system is only of use, though, if your potential customers know that you are offering the service. One of the suggested ways of doing this is to use the PayPal website to generate a special button that can then be placed on your website. This button, when clicked, will automatically allow the customer to send you the money for the item you are selling. If they don't have a PayPal account, it offers them the opportunity to get one. To do this tutorial you will need the following:

- **A PayPal account** If you are in the UK go to www.paypal.co.uk (trading in £ sterling) or get a US/International one at www.paypal.com (trading in $ dollars); at the time of writing such accounts were free to open for both individuals and businesses. You will probably need a credit card to open this account.
- **A website to install the PayPal system on** If you have not got one you can use the one provided in Appendix VI.

Selecting the Merchant Services

Log in to your new PayPal account.

Note: As this tutorial is being written about a particular website, the exact name or style of options mentioned cannot be guaranteed – PayPal may change any and all of these features. However, the principles are likely to remain the same.

Once you are logged in you will notice a tool bar along the top of the website.

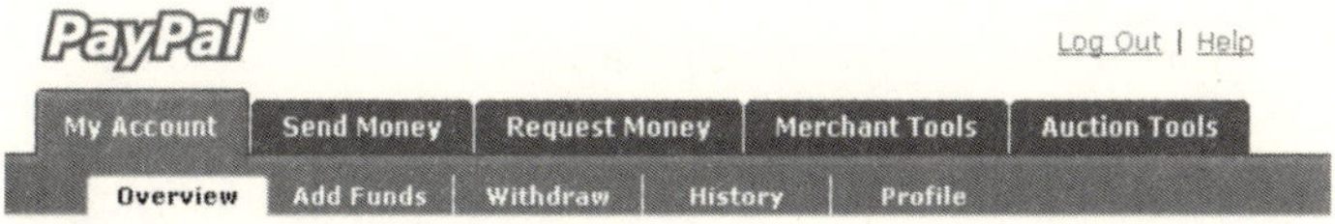

This lists your options for adding merchant abilities to a website. From this bar select 'Merchant Tools'. This will take you to a new menu screen:

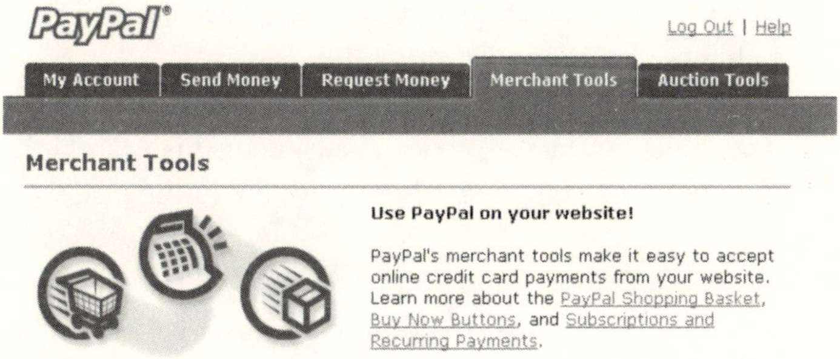

From here select the 'Buy Now Buttons' option. This will take you to a screen with information about how this system works. Once you have read this introductory information click on the 'Get Started' option:

This option will then take you to another screen where you fill in the details of how somebody visiting your site will make a payment. You will notice that there are a variety of options available – but for this we will just focus on a very simple button. The options you will need to change for this simple button are:

- **Item Name/Service** Put in the name of the film you are selling. In this example we have typed both the name of the film and the format (CD) that it is on – 'George the Mewvie CD'.
- **Item ID/Number** This is a stock reference number that you assign to your product. The way the numbering system works is totally up to you. If you planned to sell multiple items, this becomes very useful.
- **Price of Item/Service you want to sell** This is the cost of the item. In this example we have decided to charge £5 for the CD with a film on.
- **Currency** This is a drop down box containing the possible currencies you can sell in. In this example we have opted for £ sterling (as we are in the UK!).

From here, for this simple button, it is suggested you leave the rest of the options set at default (as they originally appear). The finished screen will look something like this:

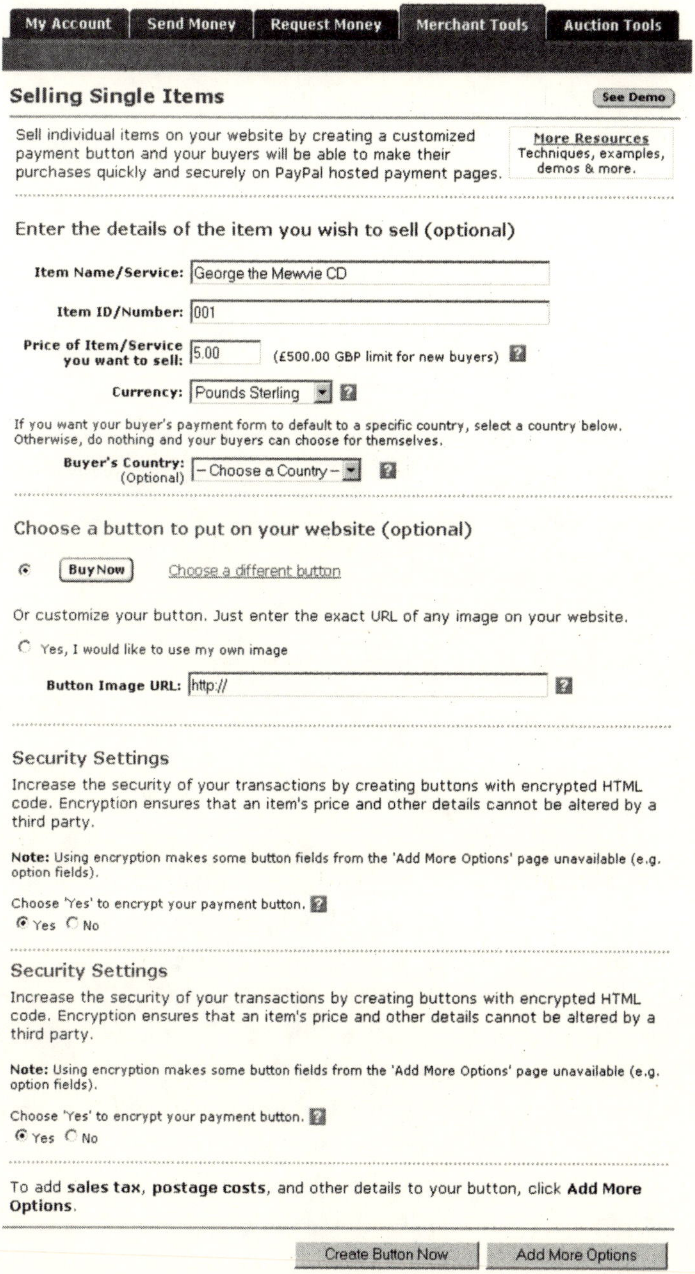

My Account | Send Money | Request Money | Merchant Tools | Auction Tools

Selling Single Items

See Demo

Sell individual items on your website by creating a customized payment button and your buyers will be able to make their purchases quickly and securely on PayPal hosted payment pages.

More Resources
Techniques, examples, demos & more.

Enter the details of the item you wish to sell (optional)

Item Name/Service: George the Mewvie CD

Item ID/Number: 001

Price of Item/Service you want to sell: 5.00 (£500.00 GBP limit for new buyers) ?

Currency: Pounds Sterling ?

If you want your buyer's payment form to default to a specific country, select a country below. Otherwise, do nothing and your buyers can choose for themselves.

Buyer's Country: (Optional) – Choose a Country – ?

Choose a button to put on your website (optional)

Buy Now   Choose a different button

Or customize your button. Just enter the exact URL of any image on your website.

Yes, I would like to use my own image

Button Image URL: http:// ?

Security Settings

Increase the security of your transactions by creating buttons with encrypted HTML code. Encryption ensures that an item's price and other details cannot be altered by a third party.

Note: Using encryption makes some button fields from the 'Add More Options' page unavailable (e.g. option fields).

Choose 'Yes' to encrypt your payment button. ?

Yes No

Security Settings

Increase the security of your transactions by creating buttons with encrypted HTML code. Encryption ensures that an item's price and other details cannot be altered by a third party.

Note: Using encryption makes some button fields from the 'Add More Options' page unavailable (e.g. option fields).

Choose 'Yes' to encrypt your payment button. ?

Yes No

To add **sales tax**, **postage costs**, and other details to your button, click **Add More Options**.

Create Button Now | Add More Options

Then click the button at the bottom marked 'Create Button Now'. This will take you to another screen where the HTML that PayPal have created to operate your button is displayed.[3] This HTML will appear as a mass of numbers, letters and symbols. This is because the default option in the creation of the button, for added security protection, encrypts all the details of the button (such as your PayPal account information – note that you do not need to know anything of how this encryption operates in order to paste this HTML into a website).[4]

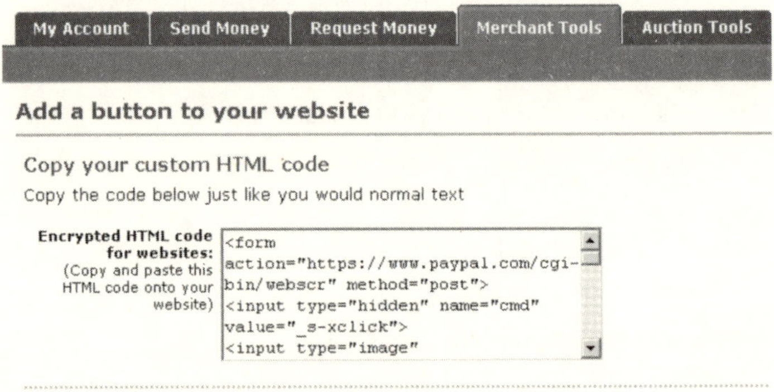
My Account
Send Money
Request Money
Merchant Tools
Auction Tools
Add a button to your website
Copy your custom HTML code
Copy the code below just like you would normal text
Encrypted HTML code for websites:
(Copy and paste this HTML code onto your website)
<form
action="https://www.paypal.com/cgi-
bin/webscr" method="post">
<input type="hidden" name="cmd"
value="_s-xclick">
<input type="image"

This HTML code needs to be copied and pasted into your website. In windows, this is done by clicking the mouse pointer in the box with the HTML, holding down the shift key and selecting all of the HTML. Once the text has been highlighted, the next step is to hold down the shift key and press the 'C' key (this copies the text to the computer's memory). Then open the file containting your webpage and while holding down the shift key, press the 'V' key (to place down the text held in the computers memory).

If you have done Appendix VI, this would involve opening the file 'index.htm' in the text editor, then scrolling down until you are almost at the end of the file and pasting the text here. This would result in HTML that looks like this:

```
<HTML>
<HEAD>
<TITLE>George the Mewvie!</TITLE>
</HEAD>
<BODY BGCOLOR=#000000 TEXT=#ffffff>
<H1>George the Mewvie – <FONT COLOR=#828282> a film about a cat!</FONT></H1><P>
<H4>George the Mewvie is a film about a cat. Not just any cat, but a special cat. The film is intended to capture the look and feel of a cats fur by allowing the compression to run riot over the footage that has been shot.</H4><P>
<H5>Contact information:
ana@pluginmanifesto.com</H5>
<P>
<IMG SRC="george_film.jpg" alt= "A still from George the Mewvie">
<P>
You can watch George the Mewvie:
<P>
<TABLE BORDER=ON>
<TR>
<TD>
If you wish to see the OpenDivX version, you can do so by logging onto to Gnutella network. Start a search for 'george' – you will get the best results if you do this on the weekend, when I am also connected to the network!
</TD>
<TD>
<A HREF=http://www.gnutella.com>Gnutella</A>
</TD>

<TR>
<TD>
If you wish to see the QuickTime version, you can do so
```

by streaming it from this site:
</TD>
<TD>
<A HREF=“george.mov”>QuickTime</A>
</TD>

<form action=“http://www.paypal.com/cgi-bin/webscr” method=“post”>
<input type=“hidden” name=“cmd” value=“_s-xclick”>
<input type=“image” src=“http://www.paypal.com/en_US/i/btn/x-click-but23.gif” border=“0” name=“submit” alt=“Make payments with PayPal – it’s fast, free and secure!”>
<input type=“hidden” name=“encrypted” value=“-----BEGIN PKCS7-----
**MIIHJwYJKoZIhvcNAQcEoIIHGDCCBxQCAQExggEwMIIBLAIBADCBlD
CBjjELMAkGA1UEBhMCVVMxCzAJBgNVBAgTAkNBMRYwFAYDVQQHEw1N
b3VudGFpbiBWaWV3MRQwEgYDVQQKEwtQYXlQYWwgSW5jLjETMBEGA1
UECxQKbGl2ZV9jZXJ0czERMA8GA1UEAxQIbGl2ZV9hcGkxHDAaBgkq
hkiG9w0BCQEWDXJlQHBheXBhbC5jb20CAQAwDQYJKoZIhvcNAQEBBQ
AEgYAnrcwZrAKtQW8RgIFeG8EkakGPcL3DqqDUn5zZRw+ezc1ju8n5
VVzA9i99x3dm7jB5C6GRJkJ3qseJJqGzCud5Flgm0XQNhokOBvOTX0
SDAznbNdkEtv+9g1Gmp+el1Z1zylRe2NEXGRxGVT831KDIEIQhnHsm
RRKapzoOzhY+djELMAkGBSsOAwIaBQAwgaQGCSqGSIb3DQEHATAUBg
gqhkiG9w0DBwQIZkGN/kGp+DSAgYAHYcNB6Hct8CxO+Ae4MdcWG4ZH**

0NkUbYBC+hrl7xG0MM4QYyrMkpiALrJmc77D9
Opp71vpLxcLpAv9AP
NTkldnF3S5nfs15buAarnl2nJZPbaxE6A6XuFA3n1P
qUdP1uL6Zmau
HSEIRPLCSU0dqs9Jc2iaveqddTZjdXa3AM7t4qCC
A4cwggODMIIC7K
ADAgECAgEAMA0GCSqGSIb3DQEBBQUAMIGO
MQswCQYDVQQGEwJVUzEL
MAkGA1UECBMCQ0ExFjAUBgNVBAcTDU1vdW
50YWluIFZpZXcxFDASBg
NVBAoTC1BheVBhbCBJbmMuMRMwEQYDVQQ
LFApsaXZlX2NlcnRzMREw
DwYDVQQDFAhsaXZlX2FwaTEcMBoGCSqGSIb3
DQEJARYNcmVAcGF5cG
FsLmNvbTAeFw0wNDAyMTMxMDEzMTVaFw0z
NTAyMTMxMDEzMTVaMIGO
MQswCQYDVQQGEwJVUzELMAkGA1UECBMC
Q0ExFjAUBgNVBAcTDU1vdW
50YWluIFZpZXcxFDASBgNVBAoTC1BheVBhbCB
JbmMuMRMwEQYDVQQL
FApsaXZlX2NlcnRzMREwDwYDVQQDFAhsaXZl
X2FwaTEcMBoGCSqGSI
b3DQEJARYNcmVAcGF5cGFsLmNvbTCBnzANBg
kqhkiG9w0BAQEFAAOB
jQAwgYkCgYEAwUdO3fxEzEtcnI7ZKZL412XvZPu
goni7i7D7prCe0A
taHTc97CYgm7NsAtJyxNLixmhLV8pyIEaiHXWAh
8fPKW+R017+EmXr
r9EaquPmsVvTywAAE1PMNOKqo2kl4Gxiz9zZqIaj
Om1fZGWcGS0f5J
Q2kBqNbvbg2/Za+GJ/qwUCAwEAAaOB7jCB6zAd
BgNVHQ4EFgQUlp98
u8ZvF71ZP1LXChvsENZklGswgbsGA1UdIwSBszC
BsIAUlp98u8ZvF7
1ZP1LXChvsENZklGuhgZSkgZEwgY4xCzAJBgNV
BAYTAlVTMQswCQYD

VQQIEwJDQTEWMBQGA1UEBxMNTW91bnRha
W4gVmlldzEUMBIGA1UECh
MLUGF5UGFsIEluYy4xEzARBgNVBAsUCmxpdm
VfY2VydHMxETAPBgNV
BAMUCGxpdmVfYXBpMRwwGgYJKoZIhvcNAQk
BFg1yZUBwYXlwYWwuY2
9tggEAMAwGA1UdEwQFMAMBAf8wDQYJKoZIhv
cNAQEFBQADgYEAgV86
VpqAWuXvX6Oro4qJ1tYVIT5DgWpE692Ag422H7y
RIr/9j/iKG4Thia
/Oflx4TdL+IFJBAyPK9v6zZNZtBgPBynXb048hsP1
6l2vi0k5Q2JKi
PDsEfBhGI+HnxLXEaUWAcVfCsQFvd2A1sxRr67i
p5y2wwBelUecP3A
jJ+YcxggGaMIIBlgIBATCBlDCBjjELMAkGA1UEB
hMCVVMxCzAJBgNV
BAgTAkNBMRYwFAYDVQQHEw1Nb3VudGFpbiB
WaWV3MRQwEgYDVQQKEw
tQYXlQYWwgSW5jLjETMBEGA1UECxQKbGl2Z
V9jZXJ0czERMA8GA1UE
AxQIbGl2ZV9hcGkxHDAaBgkqhkiG9w0BCQEWD
XJlQHBheXBhbC5jb2
0CAQAwCQYFKw4DAhoFAKBdMBgGCSqGSIb3D
QEJAzELBgkqhkiG9w0B
BwEwHAYJKoZIhvcNAQkFMQ8XDTA0MDQwOT
EzNTUwN1owIwYJKoZIhv
cNAQkEMRYEFIT+9ehE63IOoJxr3AEkE8+mDvg
0MA0GCSqGSIb3DQEB
AQUABIGAtknc9Zi9blp8cGVJqoeFKH4HX227e1n
mtZvOzq5RiOgoI5
k/N3XSkSPvnItktKTkQWqIoKqNI/n3ZI/xr4OUXF
32yCn+1iIpX44e
uEvw8m374H6NcJNs6r+gC7fnSbCeto+qbR7dGYU
fi1lQt+GlkigFFt
rg0h1fpKPjXNSAamw=
-----END PKCS7-----

```
">
</form>

</TR>
</TABLE>
</BODY>
</HTML>
```

And a final webpage that looks something like this (though in colour):

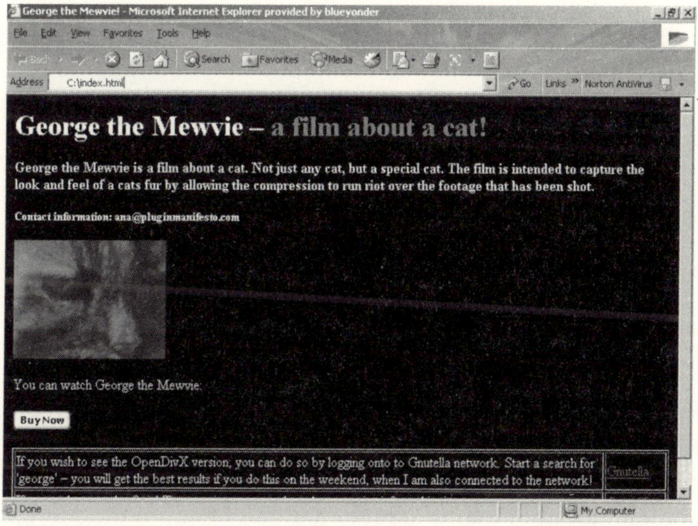

And that, as they say, is that! There are far more options available on the PayPal site: experiment and see what will suit your needs.

References and Notes

1 For more information on such scams see **http://antivirus.about.com/library/scams/blebayscam.htm**

2 **www.dSWAT.net** uses the open source commerce system

osCommerce. This system can be found at **http://www.oscommerce.com** but its installation does require a fairly high level of knowledge of server systems. Other simpler options include **http://www.ccnow.com** which is a website that allows the creation of a shop using the sites system and no technical knowledge, though you will pay a higher premium of credit card transactions and have less control.

3 For more on HTML see Appendix VI.

4 Encryption is the process of displaying information using a code so that only those with the key to the code can understand it.

Glossary

Anticopyright – takes the copyleft notion that creativity benefits from a lack of ownership and merges it with the radical political idea that 'all property is theft'.

Artifacting – blurred or pixilated patches appearing in an image where the compression technology has resulted in a noticeable loss of quality.

Audio Visual Interleaved – see AVI

AVI – Audio Visual Interleaved; a film file format that is commonly used to store such content. It is defined as being a format that adheres to the Microsoft Windows Resource Interchange File Format (RIFF) and is commonly, though not exclusively, found on Microsoft Windows machines.

Bandwidth – the amount of data that can be accessed to or from your server within a set period of time.

Broadband – this is an 'always on' connection to the internet. The bandwidth available for download is usually 512 Kbps or more depending on the service provider.

Bitsream – audio/video data 'bundled' for passage over the internet.

Buffering – the initial delay before a streaming media file plays, while the initial portion of the data is downloaded.

Byte – a measurement of data storage. This is composed of 8 'bits', an even smaller storage measurement. A kilobyte is 1024 bytes. A megabyte is 1,048,576 bytes and a gigabyte is 1,073,741,824 bytes.

Capture Card – the name given to a device, often installed inside the computer, that provides an additional port for the camera etc. to connect through.

Codec – compression/decompression tool, bundling up data in order to send it, and reassembling the data when it arrives.

Compression – the name given to the various techniques that are used to make digital files smaller.

Copyright – the placing of fixed legal boundaries around the output of a creative process.

Copyleft – a way to license a work so that unrestricted redistribution, copying and modification is permitted, provided that all copies and derivatives retain the exact same licensing.

Data rate – the amount of data that is transferred every second.

Default – the settings that a piece of software or hardware comes with to begin with. To restore the default is to reset things to how they were set initially by the manufacturer.

DivX – Media player made by DivXNetworks Inc.

DV – Digital Video

DVD – Digital Video Disk

Encoding – the process of compressing film footage using an appropriate software package, i.e. QuickTime Pro.

Encryption – the process of displaying information using a code so that only those with the key to the code can understand it.

Establishing Shot – an opening view onto a scene that places the narrative within time and space.

Export – the name given to the process of creating a version of a film, song etc. that can then exist on its own without the need of the software in which is created.

Fairshare – a method of using copyleft ideas in action to fund a project using a combination of investment and donation.

Fan Fiction – creative work authored by a fan about existing intellectual property.

File Trade Network – see Peer-to-Peer Network.

Films Not Made for, but Distributed Via the Internet – a film taking advantage of the internet for distribution purposes.

Filter – processes applied to footage, image or sound to create an interesting outcome; the filter may change the colour, the contrast or add any number of interesting effects.

FireWire – a method of connecting digital devices together, often a camera and computer, based on the IEEE 1394 standard.

FSF – Free Software Foundation. The group championing the cause of free software ideas.

GIF – Graphics Interchange Format, a form of compression used for images.

Gigabyte – see Byte.

GNN – Guerrilla News Network

Hardrive – the component of your computer that acts as the permanent storage space. It is normally measured in gigabytes.

Host – the name given to the server containing a specific website.

HTML – Hyper Text Mark-up Language, the scripting language that websites are written in.

IP – Intellectual Property (can also mean Internet Protocol, see TCP/IP).

Import – the name given to the process of bringing in a file (film footage, sound etc.) into the working area of a piece of software so it can be used.

Interframe Compression – compression technology that is applied between frames.

Intraframe Compression – compression technology applied to a single image.

ISMA – Internet Streaming Media Alliance, a streaming technology lobby group.

Keyframe – a frame containing all of the necessary bits of movie information, while subsequent frames contain only the information that has changed.

kHz – kilohertz is the name given to a unit of measurement for sound frequencies. Its exact meaning is that 1kHz represents one thousand cycles per second.

Kilobyte – see Byte.

Kilohertz – see kHz

Layering – the placing of one or more layers of footage on top of another, to be played at the same time, with a varying degree of transparency, to create interesting effects.

Live – in internet terms, this refers to a file being made publicly accessible.

Lossless Compression – compression that is reversible and so can restore the compressed data to its original uncompressed form.

Lossy Compression – compression that is non-reversible and so cannot restore the compressed data back to its original uncompressed form.

Machinima – where the technology used to create a 3D computer game is re-used as a virtual studio to create films.

Media Player – a software program that plays a streamed or downloaded version of a music or film (or even game) file on a computer.

Megabyte – see Byte.

Meta Data – a name sometimes used to refer to the additional text information (such as director, film company etc.) or Movie Information, which is added to a file. Also used in HTML.

Modem – a device that passes data to and from phone lines to allow your computer to connect to the internet.

MP3 – Mpeg-1 Audio Layer-3, reduced (or compressed) form of music.

MPEG – Moving Pictures Experts Group, both a group setting compression standards and the name used for their compression technology, e.g. MPEG-4 video or JEP images.

Mplayer – an Open Source media player.

Open Source – an ideology that has no faith in the idea of copyright. Practitioners make all the programming code that they produce free for everyone to use and modify, provided any new users then adhere to the same ideals.

Operating System – the name given to the software system that your computer runs. Typically this will be Microsoft Windows, Mac OS or Linux.

PDA or Personal Digital Assistant – a tiny portable PC that offers much of the staple functionality of a computer, such as an address book, email system, diary, calculator and so on. Increasingly, they are being used to deliver entertainment too; including games, films and music.

Peer-to-Peer Network (also File Trade Network) – a system that acts as a go-between enabling users to view and exchange files. Examples include Napster, Kazaa and Gnutella.

Personal Digital Assistant – see PDA.

Pixel – the smallest recognizable element of a digital image, a tiny dot of a single colour. When a film or image is described as being, for example, 640 x 480, this means it is 640 pixels across by 480 pixels down.

pluginmanifesto – a document aimed at creating a definitive framework that filmmakers can use to produce films specifically for the internet.

Processor – the name given to the brain of a computer. The more powerful a processor, the faster the machine will run – but only if the other components, such as the RAM, can keep up!

QuickTime – media player made by Apple.

RAM – Random Access Memory. The working memory of your computer. The higher this figure is, the more temporary space your computer has to perform processes and calculations and so the faster it will run.

RealPlayer – media player made by RealNetworks.

Redundancy – the common elements within a body of data.

RIAA – Recording Industry Association of America. The principal US music industry lobby group.

Rushes – the name given to the raw footage taken during the shoot.

Shot Reverse Shot – establishing a link between two things in separate shots by placing the shots next to each other through the editing process.

TCP/IP – Transmission Control Protocol/ Internet Protocol, the system the internet uses as a communication language.

Temperature – in filmmaking, refers to the warm or cold look of the lighting.

TGA or Truevision Targa – the name given to a format developed by Truevision Inc (now called Pinnacle Systems) to store the position and colour details of each pixel in an image.

Timeline – a bar representing the length of the footage. There is normally an accompanying slider on the timeline to indicate where on this line the user is currently viewing.

Timeout – when the process of transferring data or maintaining an internet/network connection is left waiting for the next bit of information for so long that the process is re-set.

Traditional Promotion – a digitized version of films shot with the same production methods and technology used for TV/Cinema.

URL – Uniform Resource Locator, or web address.

USB – Universal Serial Bus is a method of connecting digital devices. There are two versions: USB and the more powerful USB 2.0.

Web Film – a film made with the medium of the internet and its constraints in mind.

Winamp – media player made by Nullsoft.

Windows Media Player – media player made by Microsoft.

Wizard – the name given to a step-by-step dialogue box intended to guide the user though a process in an easier manner.

Index

A
Advertising, 38, 67-9, 70
Amerika, Mark, 152, 161
Anticopyright, 49, 53-4, 57, 144, 154
Analogue, 108-113, 117, 119
Anarchist, 54
Animation, 11, 23, 101, 107, 110, 114
Apple, 37, 39-42, 97, 112, 122, 134, 141, 205-211
Artifacting, 128, 131, 158
AtomFilms, 23, 60, 68, 72, 144

B
Bandwidth, 79, 82, 139, 141, 145, 151, 154, 207, 208
BBC, 36, 45, 65, 78, 80, 85, 152, 161
BetaMax, 37, 43, 45
Bitstream, 40
Broadband, 31, 65, 96, 144, 155, 156, 208
Buffering, 137
Byte, 19, 25, 115, 116, 136, 180, 206

C
Capture Card, 116
CD, 13, 25, 29-31, 67, 232
CD-ROM, 40, 117
Codec, 32, 40, 44, 83, 104, 137, 146, 155, 197-204
Compression, 25, 31, 40, 83, 89, 95, 100, 104, 125-134, 139, 155-8, 173, 195, 205-211
Copyright, 24-30, 47-60, 63, 66, 144, 196
Copyleft, 48, 51-3, 56-9, 81, 84, 144

D
D, Chuck, 29
Data rate, 208-9
Decompression, 40, 125-134
Digital Video – see DV
Documentary, 29, 69, 78, 85
DOGME 95, 75-8, 83, 85, 121, 121,
Distribution, 13, 15, 21, 25-8, 30, 31, 52, 77, 80, 96-7, 142-4, 197-204
DivX, 32-5, 41-2, 45, 198-204, 224, 225, 227, 237
DivXNetwork, 33, 45
DV, 93, 99, 101, 107, 108, 109, 113, 117, 120, 121, 183-195
DVGate, 175, 183-195

E
Editing, 93-5, 101, 108, 109, 111-115, 183-195
Encode, 132, 137, 204, 208-10, 222
Establishing Shot, 155

F
Fairshare, 66-7, 72, 74
Fan Fiction, 58
File Size, 25, 151, 180, 125-134, 207-9
File Trade Network – see Peer-to-Peer Network
Films Not Made For But Distributed Via The Internet, 19
Filter, 84, 94-5, 101, 172, 191
FireWire, 110, 114-6, 118-9,122-3, 177
Flash, 23, 79, 83, 85, 101, 107, 110-11, 174, 177
Free Software Foundation – see FSF
FTP, 140, 145, 147
FSF, 28, 33-4, 59

G
GIF, 118, 145, 222
Gigabyte – see Byte
GNN, 69-73
Gnucleus, 145, 148, 198-203
Gnutella, 143, 145, 148, 197-203, 224-9
Grammatron, 152, 161
Guerrilla News Network – see GNN

H
Hancock, Hugh, 159, 162
Hardrive, 112, 116
Host, 65, 135-46, 228

I
Indymedia, 80, 86, 153, 161-2
Intellectual Property – see IP
IP, 55-8
Interframe Compression, 130-133
Intraframe Compression, 127-9, 133
Internet Streaming Media Alliance – see ISMA
ISMA, 40

K
Kazaa, 68, 142-4

L
Linux, 39, 51-2, 112, 140
Lossless Compression, 109, 117, 125-134
Lossy Compression, 125-134
Lynch, David, 65

M
Machinima, 159, 160-2
Macromedia, 68, 85, 105, 110, 117, 147
Manovich, Lev, 11-15
Marshall, Stephen, 69, 70, 72, 75
Media Player, 32, 38-45, 95-96, 113, 131, 137, 140, 196

MP3, 25-34, 40, 45, 131, 195
MPEG, 25, 39, 44, 113, 131, 133, 141, 198, 205-6, 211
MPEG-1, 25, 39
MPEG-2, 40
MPEG-4, 40, 113, 141, 198
Mplayer, 45
Muybridge, Eadweard, 159, 161-2

N

Napster, 26-34

O

Operating System, 17, 39, 112, 144, 148, 198

P

PDA, 148
Peer-to-Peer Network, 27-33, 96, 142-7, 198, 202
Pixel, 107, 117, 194
Post-production, 93, 94-5, 100, 111-115
Pre-production, 92-3, 100-102
Production,15, 43, 63, 91-2, 93-6, 102-3

Q

QuickTime, 40, 42, 92, 113, 115, 131, 133, 141, 147, 162, 222, 226, 205-211
QuickTime Pro, 130, 183, 194, 205-211

R

RAM, 112, 115, 118
Reality TV, 78-9
Recording Industry Association of America – see RIAA
RIAA, 28, 29, 30, 63, 144, 148
Rodriguez, Robert, 113, 117, 118, 155
Rota, Jerome, 32
Rubio, Kevin, 18
Rushes, 94

S

Script, 92, 101, 104, 169-176
Shoot, 23, 93, 94, 101, 106, 119-121
Shooting Schedule, 93, 101
Sony, 17, 37
Sound, 94-5, 114, 115, 121-3, 179-180, 190, 193-5, 208-9
Stateless Approach, 136
Storyboard, 94, 111, 164, 169-176
Streaming, 17, 19, 23, 40-3, 44, 64-5, 136-7, 140-2, 146, 147
Streaming Approach, 136, 137
StreamWorks, 17
Stallman, Richard, 28, 43, 45, 59, 66, 71, 73, 204
Stutz, Michael, 51-2, 59, 85

T
TCP/IP, 135
Television, 13, 61, 65, 74, 78-80
Temperature, 120
Timeline, 108, 186-190
Timeout, 151, 161
Traditional Promotion, 19
Treatment, 50, 92, 101
Tripod, 93, 120
TV – see Television

U
URL, 135
USB, 114, 119, 122, 123

V
Van Petten, Vince, 31
VHS, 37-43, 45, 108, 110, 117, 121
VirtualDub, 94, 112, 118
VirtualDubMod, 112, 116, 118, 183-195

W
Welles, Orson, 99, 104
White, Mike, 47-8, 58
Winamp, 42, 44
Windows Media Player, 32, 44, 131, 140
Winzip, 126, 133
Wizard, 132, 134

X
Xing Technology, 17-18, 22, 23

Z
Zoom, 117